D0582482

COVENTRY LIBRARIES

Who beat the ALL the BLACKS?

Who beat the ALL the BLACKS?

ALUN GIBBARD

y Lolfa

I fy rhieni, am adael i fi weld y gêm
... llawer mwy

Coventry City Council	
APL	
3 8002 02089 455 8	
Askews & Holts	May-2013
796.333094	£9.95

First impression: 2012

© Copyright Alun Gibbard and Y Lolfa Cyf., 2012

The contents of this book are subject to copyright, and may not be reproduced by any means, mechanical or electronic, without the prior, written consent of the publishers.

The publishers wish to acknowledge the support of Cyngor Llyfrau Cymru

Max Boyce '9–3' words, by kind permission of EMI

ISBN: 978 184771 469 5

FSC

Published and printed in Wales
on paper from well maintained forests by
Y Lolfa Cyf., Talybont, Ceredigion SY24 5HE
website www.ylolfa.com
e-mail ylolfa@ylolfa.com
tel 01970 832 304
fax 832 782

Contents

Preface

THE NEWSPAPERS WERE all saying pretty much the same thing: London 2012 was the chance for Britain to show what it was made of. It was a message that transcended sport and told the world what we were really like. Putting aside definitions of what 'British' really meant, a disparate collection of journalists from unconnected papers, knew that sport was something other than just results, performances and personal bests. It got to the heart of a nation's identity.

We know all about that in Wales. Rugby tells the world who we are and what we are. In countries where rugby is played, Wales exists. This book is about one club game forty years ago to this Olympic year, which said much about sport, identity and Wales.

First and foremost it was one amazing rugby achievement. The small town of Llanelli in west Wales produced a team which beat the mighty All Blacks. In setting to put this story of that match together, there was one obvious thing at the top of my wish list: to get to speak to as many of the men on the pitch that day as possible. Fourteen are still with us and everyone has contributed to this book and been extremely supportive in doing so. I can't thank them enough: Roger, Andy, J.J., Roy, Phil, Chico, Hefin, Gareth, Tommy, Derek, Delme, Tony, Roy and Barry have been easy to talk to and unassuming in the telling of their epic feat. It's obvious that those 80 minutes have inspired these men for forty years. Thanks also to Roy Bergiers for giving myself and photographer Emyr Young an excuse to behave like schoolboys again and have a little throw around of the original match ball in Owens Sports, Carmarthen. We didn't need any encouragement! Thanks to Emyr for his photographs in this book, and for his support. And a big thank you to Mark Lloyd.

The one man on the bench whose story is in this book is reserve scrum half Selwyn Williams. The reason why he is the only sub I have spoken to will become apparent, and I thank Selwyn for agreeing to share his particular story. It's not always easy to share what it's like to be left out. Apologies to Meirion Davies, Gwyn Ashby, Chris Charles, Bryan Llewelyn and Alan James, the other subs on that day, who contributed so much to the preparation and the occasion.

The presence of two greats, who have left us in the intervening forty years, loom large on these pages too. Grav and Carwyn James became legends in their own right in Welsh public life following 1972. Their memories of the game are taken from their writings and comments made to the Llanelli team members.

People from outside the club have their say as well. Max Boyce, Huw Llewelyn Davies, Clive Rowlands and Peter Stead testify to the wider impact of that win, crossing as it did the Loughor bridge, and then spreading throughout Wales and the rugby world. Their observations lie side by side with the story of the people of Llanelli who were part of the day: the three lads changing the scoreboard, committee man Marlston Morgan and photographer Alan Richards, for example. Alan Richards' photographs are included in this book and are an invaluable contribution to the story of the day. Special thanks go to Les Williams, who was the club historian until this year and who has had a long association with rugby in Llanelli. He has been invaluable in providing facts and figures and a few mementos too. Diolch, Les. Many thanks to Peter Stead for his interest in this project and kindly agreeing to read the book before it was published – any historical inaccuracies still left are my own. Thanks also to Jean Jones, for permission to use a poem composed by her late husband, Dic Jones.

I was also keen to hear a New Zealand perspective on the game and I set about tracking down star winger Bryan

Williams, now the president of his country's rugby union. Thanks to Derek Quinnell as go-between, many emails were exchanged before one arrived from Bryan telling me that he was on tour with the All Blacks in Argentina. He would be free in his hotel in Buenos Aires that afternoon and was happy for me to phone him for a chat. That's what happened and I must confess to being a little awestruck while talking to him. He was extremely co-operative and his contribution to this book is greatly appreciated.

In all, over forty interviews were conducted for this book in order to understand what that victory meant to both the club and the town, and how the rest of Wales rejoiced as well. All this is put in the context of how rugby started in the town more than a century ago and the link between the sport and the industry which shaped the town. Public schools and foundries came together 140 years ago when both Llanelli and Llanelli RFC were established. The date of the All Blacks game in 1972 was given as the centenary of the Llanelli club – whether it actually was or not will be discussed in these pages – but that was also the period which was at the end of the industrial tradition which gave birth to the club.

As an avid rugby fan, I was lucky enough to be commissioned to write this book. By the time I was writing the last chapters, I had moved to live, ironically, within a stone's throw of the ground where the victory happened. In '72 I was at the game myself, as a pupil of Llanelli Boys' Grammar School. At that time I was a twelve-year-old living in Bynea with my parents and sisters, Menna and Nia. Since then David has joined the family and my three wonderful nieces, Beth, Lowri and Ffion have grown up to enjoy rugby – having strong links with Newport, Cardiff and Llanelli, they are spoilt for choice! I thank my family for their support in all things. It's because of my parents I am able to say 'I was there' in '72, and that's why this book is dedicated to them. That's where the story starts.

Alun Gibbard
October 2012

1

My game

'... maybe rugby simply brings out the best in people. It's a chicken and egg situation. Does rugby simply attract the sort of person whose friendship and qualities I enjoy or does the game itself – the actual physical confrontation and challenges it presents – help mould or create these people? There is an instant recognition between rugby people...'

Richard Harries,
Hollywood star, Munsterman, avid rugby fan

IT WAS A day that seemed would never come. I knew all about the All Blacks. I knew they had been beaten in a Test series by the British and Irish Lions in 1971. But the fuss made because of that victory made it obvious that the Lions had beaten a special team, and on their own soil. I could feel the effect that their anticipated arrival was having on our little town. I hadn't felt it before, even though the Queen or Prince Charles had driven past our very front door only a few years before with much pomp and circumstance. The fact I can't remember which member of the Royal family came so close to our house says it all. But, at 12 years old, I knew the names of the All Black squad before they even left New Zealand to come to my hometown.

Not long before that, as I crossed from a single figure to a double figure age, my father had taken me to see my first live game at Stradey. I stood with men and boys, women and girls, on the legendary Tanner Bank. I have no idea who was playing for Llanelli or against them. But I had been to a game and my father had taken me. It was a rite of passage. I had stood shoulder to knee with grown men at Stradey Park. The Scarlets were divinity, all fifteen of them, individually, and as one. They were up there with Adam West's *Batman*, Richard Greene's *Robin Hood* and Ron Ely's *Tarzan*.

Imagine the sheer delight of knowing then that it was within the realms of possibility that I'd get a ticket to see my gods play the mighty All Blacks. When that ticket actually arrived, it was unspeakable joy. It meant more than winning a Llanelli schools' essay competition when I was 8; more than getting the *Thunderbirds* suit I had craved for so long; more than finishing that paint-by-numbers of a Native American chief's head; more than sneaking that first peck on the primary school yard and more than playing Joseph in the nativity play – the minister's son always played Joseph anyway! All that was kids' stuff.

I had no idea what was ahead of me, of course. But the expectation alone was greater than any reality I had experienced in my twelve-and-a-bit years on earth. When the day finally came I was beside myself. That was actually a tricky state for me to be in, as too much excitement usually meant an asthma attack. So I had to be carefully excited, and show contained enthusiasm. But it didn't work. I was like a spinning top, running round the house shouting Scarlets! Scarlets! at the top of my voice, with my scarf held high above my head.

I was picked up by my friend's father to be driven to the match. We parked in the town centre and walked the two miles to Stradey. Even with legs barely two feet long, that was no problem. As I walked I'd never seen so many people. There were hordes coming out of every street. It was, to be honest, a little frightening, as spasms of anxiety shot through me from time to time. The sheer mass of people thronging from all directions was completely overwhelming.

Ahead next was Stradey Park itself. People packed into the Stand, the Pwll End, the Town or Scoreboard End and the infamous Tanner Bank; noise moved around indiscriminately: north, south, east and west. My little eyes darted restlessly here, there and everywhere trying to take it all in. Then it became obvious where we were supposed to sit. Utter disbelief. There was a narrow line of wooden benches stretching all along the touchline in front of the Tanner Bank, towards the Pwll End. I would be sitting on a wooden bench only a few feet away from the touchline with hundreds of other schoolchildren. For me that was an extra bonus. Usually I watched rugby games in between bits of people's bodies, through a crooked arm here, a sideways lean there, finding gaps between people wherever possible. Now, the whole pitch opened up in front of me, nothing between me and the thirty men who would be playing. The best view in the world, ever! The only possible thing blocking my view would be when the touch judge – that's what they called them in those days – ran in front of me. I actually would see the whole game. This certainly was a day of new emotions and experiences.

When the game started, I'd never experienced such a buzz. The sound of feet on the turf was like the thunder of buffalos that cowboys in the Wild West would have heard across the plains. The sound of every tackle felt as if it should be accompanied by the 'Biff' and 'Pow' cartoon bubble exclamations that Batman and Robin provoked on their TV series. I didn't know these words at the time, but it was the most sensory, explosive game I had ever seen.

Every now and then, I would look away from the action and the excitement on the pitch and along the touchline to the area behind the dead ball line at the Town End. There, in a neat row, were three or four blue three-wheeler disabled cars, dwarfed by the crowds in the Scoreboard End. My grandfather was in one of them. I felt a swelling of pride as I looked across the crowds and connected with my grandfather, even though neither of us could see each other across the length of the pitch amongst such a crowd. As a fireman laying explosives in a coal seam, he'd suffered a serious accident underground in a Pontyberem coal mine just after World War II. He'd fractured his spine, lost half a leg, as well as suffering serious internal damage.

He was both special to me personally, and representative of something far bigger. Also in the crowd was his son, my father, although I had no idea where he was! This was a crowd of working people, miners, tin workers, car industry employees, factory workers, teachers, preachers, doctors and dentists – and children. It was a crowd full of grandfathers, fathers and grandsons, grandmothers, mothers and daughters – sharing.

But of course it got more special. Llanelli won. I was on the pitch before the final whistle had stopped reverberating around a rapturous Stradey. I stretched to my full height to give captain Delme Thomas a huge congratulatory slap on his back – and promptly stung my little hand on his muscular hide. I was soon swamped and I moved out to the safety of the touchline under the stand as soon as was practically possible. The feelings were quite overwhelming.

One thing still haunts me about that game to this day. Before leaving the house that morning, I went to the toilet near our back door. As I stood there, still singing and chanting, I changed the lyrics of the chant I had sung all morning. At the top of my voice, I started singing melodically the tune of 'Amazing Grace': nine three, nine three, nine three, nine three. I had bought a single of the Welsh-language version of that hymn, 'Pererin Wyf', sung by Welsh singer Iris Williams, not long before the game and played it often when I wasn't listening to Pink Floyd or Welsh singer Meic Stevens' 'Brawd Houdini'. Was it divine intervention to plant those numbers in my mind and to sing them to that tune? I'll never know but that probably is pushing it a bit!

However, the fact that I sang those words is unquestionable. It's true and no one will convince me otherwise this side of the grave. They'll have a bit of a job the other side too!

So, like thousands of people on that day, I can say that I was there. But there's more to it than the accumulative experiences of fans relishing a historic victory. Why has this game captured the imagination so much? Welsh club sides have registered nearly thirty victories against the big three countries: South

Africa, New Zealand and Australia over the years. But this one, when Llanelli beat the All Blacks 9–3 on 31 October 1972, stands out. And not just in Llanelli, as the shock waves spread throughout south Wales and beyond, inspiring Max Boyce to write a new song as well. In addition to reliving that day, the run-up to it and the euphoria after it, looking for an answer to the question 'Why this game?' is part of this book's intention. But that wasn't the question on a twelve-year-old's mind forty years ago!

2

The new game

Llanelli is a town whose Welsh credentials are difficult to match. In its economic heyday, it was a heavily industrialised cauldron of working-class Welshness, truly one of the most remarkable towns in Wales.

Huw Edwards, *The Story of Wales*

ON A MATCH day full of passion and aggression, with the partisan crowd in fine voice, it's hard to believe that there was a time when rugby didn't exist in Llanelli. Such a thought would have been totally inconceivable on an October day in 1972 when the town's fifteen heroes conquered the might of the world's premier rugby nation, New Zealand. That day it was as if rugby itself could not have been invented anywhere else other than this small town in a corner of Wales.

In those prehistoric days before rugby, the town was very different. It was a small rural settlement which was changing into a larger industrial place. A century before Llanelli Rugby Club was formed, the whole town boasted no greater a population than would go to see the Scarlets play in an away match in France today. In the intervening century, coal pits were sunk, foundries established, copper and tin works opened. In a period of five years before the beginning of the nineteenth century, the population had already grown by two and a half thousand. It would continue to grow as each decade of the nineteenth century unfolded.

With the new century barely a few years old, the new Llanelli and Mynydd Mawr Railway hurtled along newly-laid tracks in this corner of Carmarthenshire. That was 1803 and it was used for industry along with horse-drawn carriages of coal to, amongst other places, the Stradey Iron Works. In 1839, steam engines replaced horses, and a new railway line between Llanelli and Pontarddulais was established. This line carried coal to the New Dock in Llanelli, and the New Dock Stars became one of the region's prominent rugby teams. The area was opening up. The railway linked initially to Llandeilo, and then to Swansea. Soon, these railway tracks would bring all sorts of people in from hitherto unimagined places and would take local workers to find labour in far off fields.

People didn't take all the developments unquestioningly. There were signs of unrest on the roads as gangs called Rebecca's daughters (men dressed as women) would riot and smash tollgates to protest against the landowners and their road charges. People were unhappy and beginning to find their own voice.

In the middle of all this pioneering heavy industry, the gentler, but no less industrious, Llanelly Pottery flourished, bringing masters of that craft from its better-known heartland in Staffordshire. Later on, these new workers wouldn't understand the new game with a funny shaped ball, and were instrumental in starting Llanelli Football Club. It wasn't just the pottery that the boys from Stoke helped the Llanelli people with.

People had started to come together in new ways and for new reasons, as they had also done so in many other places right across south Wales. In Llanelli, the workers came together in the pits, the tin works and the copper works. Llanelli soon became the town which provided up to half of the world's tinplate, earning the town its nickname, Tinopolis. The area between Llanelli and Aberavon produced 90 per cent of Britain's copper at one time. Ten years before Llanelli Rugby Club was formed, the docks at Llanelli were responsible for importing half of Britain's lead ore. This area was the world's centre for the non-ferrous metal industry for half of the century, and led to the formation of so many local rugby clubs. There was, indeed, a Welsh way of smelting ore, recognised worldwide.

Men packed into these new foundries and pits. The danger kept them together, the dust settled indiscriminately on each lung. This influx and industry brought with it a darker side, of course. Cholera blighted the town at the start of the 1830s, and a few years later a workhouse was built not far from where Parc y Scarlets stands today. Nothing stood still for long in the years leading up to the formation of Llanelli Rugby Club. It was the genesis of a mass society, in an area where sheep and cows had dominated previously.

These people worshipped in the new grand chapels which stood proud in the thick, shifting smoke which belched and wisped out of factory chimneys. There were dozens of chapels. And the men drank together of course. There were plenty of pubs in the area and their number grew and grew as more workers moved in. Many of these pubs were drunk dry when the Scarlets beat the All Blacks. And, thanks to an iron and tinplate works' owner, not only were the pubs mushrooming in the town, but there was also a brewery too, which still stands and still brews. Up until then, each pub tended to brew and sell its own beer. An industrial enterprise turned into a commercial enterprise when a man who came into the area to put his money into heavy industry, put some of his profits into satisfying the sweaty thirst his workplace had created. So now, one brewery served many pubs. Later on, Felinfoel Brewery was the first in Britain and only the second in the world to put beer in cans. These cans even found their way to the front line of a world war, to ease a soldier's torment. Felinfoel was soon followed by the town's other big brewery, Buckleys, founded by a Methodist minister from the north of England. A pint of the Reverend James can still be enjoyed today.

That first rugby team was established and developed in a

Llanelli which was creating a new identity. Rugby and identity still resonate in twenty-first-century Wales. Llanelli then had a new confidence, as is seen in the chapel architecture which still stands proud in the town's centre today; as is also seen in the innovative spirit that gave it the drive to forge a name for itself in the industrial world across the Loughour bridge and far beyond; as is seen in its distinctive pottery and the invention of the world's first spare wheel – the Stepney spare wheel – which kept the wheels of industry and leisure turning in so many developing industrial countries around the world.

The Stepney spare wheel was invented by Thomas Morris Davies in Llanelli in 1904 at a time when cars were manufactured without spare wheels. A puncture was an event dreaded by all drivers. Morris and his brother opened a factory in Llanelli and by 1909 their catalogue proudly claimed that Stepney spare wheels were fitted to all London taxis. In 1922 the company became Stepney Tyres Ltd. and moved from Llanelli to Walthamstow. Car makers soon cottoned on to this invention and all new cars now had spare wheels. But the Stepney name lived on. A Stepney is still the everyday name for a spare wheel in India, Bangladesh, Malta and Brazil. The word has even passed into common language in parts of India, where a person who is regarded of not much use at work is called a Stepney! The gentrified landowners who went under the name of Stepney in Llanelli would probably turn in their graves if they realised their surname was used in this way today!

Klondike was another name soon heard on the lips of the townspeople of Llanelli when the rugby club was into its third decade. That was the name they affectionately used for the giant Llanelli Steel Works which opened in 1907. There certainly wasn't any gold in them there mills, but it was a mass employer which put food on the table for generations of Llanelli people and bought them quite a few pints of Buckleys or Felinfoel too. The Klondike would play its own part in that famous 1972 victory, as we shall learn later.

The people of this new Llanelli worked hard, worshipped hard, drank hard and they then, of course, needed to play hard. The big leisure craze in Llanelli towards the end of the Victorian age was cycling. It had a massive appeal in the town. Boxing, with or without gloves, drew huge crowds in the fairgrounds of south Wales, and Llanelli was no exception. The Queensbury Rules, boxing's time honoured and much respected code of conduct which moved the sport on from its bare knuckle days, were in fact written by J.G. Chambers from Llanelli. No doubt the pugilistic powers that be thought that the Marquis of Queensbury rules sounded grander than the Chambers of Llanelli rules.

Not long after Llanelli Rugby Club was formed, a stadium was built on land now part of Parc y Scarlets to accommodate the new sports of cycling and running. Football matches were also played there and boxing tournaments were always popular. It's reported that 10,000 people came to see Gypsy Daniels fight at this County Athletic Ground. It had opened to huge fanfares following a fundraising campaign by the owners of two local cycling shops. This sporting stadium attracted other businesses too, such as the opening of the Halfway Hotel which today caters for the needs of match day rugby fans on their way to see Scarlet heroes play today.

But the County Athletic Ground also faced local opposition as well, with clergy expressing fears about the barbaric nature of boxing, for example. They vehemently protested when the official opening ceremony of the ground was held on an Easter weekend. Many townspeople also opposed its opening because it was too far from the town centre. How ironic that much of the opposition to the location of Parc y Scarlets on the same site in the first decade of the twenty-first century was based on exactly the same argument.

So people came together to enjoy a variety of sports. They congregated in darkened buildings too, to watch moving images on a big screen. Cinema pioneer and film-maker, William Haggar, not only brought his touring cinema this far west, but opened a permanent one in the town too. The town was the home of Wales' first silent movie star, Gareth Hughes. He was born not far from Parc y Scarlets and at one time received a higher billing than Rudolph Valentino.

But there was this new sport too – rugby. It was established a world away from the gritty reality of industrial Llanelli, at a public school in England, or so the story goes. The truth might be a little different. Llanelli was not in the same world as the town of Rugby where the game developed, even if it didn't begin there. What was it about this rugby game? Maybe it was tailor-made for men who were already joined at the hip in the male culture of heavy industry – they were already team mates while working in the furnaces and on coal faces. Maybe this new team sport was just for them.

Rugby came to this ever-changing area directly from the town that gave it its name. Two of Llanelli's new industrialists, Morewood and Rogers, had at the beginning of the 1870s, established not only new centres of heavy industry but new processes as well. Some of Morewood's ancestors had fought with the House of York in the Wars of the Roses and an ancestor of Rogers was the first one to be martyred by Queen Mary, the original Bloody Mary.

They had both pioneered the process of galvanising tinned iron, which Morewood had developed while living in New Jersey, USA. When they came to Llanelli they established the Marsh Iron Works, which became the Marshfield Works, then the Western Tinplate Works. The Marshfield Tap pub still opens its doors today. They also opened the South Wales Works at Machynys, the Yspitty Tinplate Works in Bynea on the eastern outskirts of the town, as well as the Baglan Works in Britton Ferrry, near Neath and works in Cwmbwrla near Swansea, in addition to their American ventures.

When Rogers died, his wife was keen to find work for their son John. By that time, Morewood was the largest and most successful tinplate works' owner in Britain and living in Llangennech, a small village on the outskirts of Llanelli.

John Rogers went to live with him in 1872. That turned out to be a very significant move indeed.

John Rogers had been a pupil at Rugby School between 1863 and 1866. When he moved to Llanelli, he brought with him the game which he'd learned there. Indeed he brought the funny shaped ball with him as well. As comedian Peter Cook put it, with tongue firmly planted in his cheek no doubt, 'Rugby is a game for the mentally deficient... That is why it was invented by the British. Who else but an Englishman would invent an oval ball?'

There was even a link with Rugby Public School on the field of play on 31 October 1972. Winger Andy Hill, one of the point scorers that day, had a brother who was a mathematics teacher at Rugby School for 18 years. Andy relates his brother saying that they were told at the school that the word for grounding the ball over the line came from a games' master's comment on the occasion when William Webb Ellis picked up the football and ran with it. The master's response was, 'That wasn't a goal young man, but it was a good try!' Hence the word 'try' for grounding the ball over the goal line.

The first record we have of rugby being played in Llanelli is of the young John Rogers having a kick-about with some friends in People's Park in the middle of the town. Rogers went on to try to establish a rugby club in the town. He gathered like-minded people together and a meeting was held on 11 November 1875 in the Athenaeum, where the town library stands today. In an upstairs room thirty people met with Rogers in the chair. They played their first game on 1 January 1876. A team of four backs and nine forwards, local businessmen and tinplate workers side by side, took on the Cambrian Club from Swansea.

It really was a case of jumpers marking goalposts in those early days and the pitch in People's Park stretched from one end of the park to the other. Llanelli played in blue, their jerseys had high collars, and they wore tight trousers to well under the knee. And, for some reason, they wore Tam O'Shanter type hats with a tassel coming down over the ear! Luckily, that fashion didn't catch on. The team first played in scarlet in 1884, when they played an Irish XV on their way home from Cardiff after playing Wales.

Disaster struck at the end of the 1875/76 season when the club captain, Arthur Buchanan, was accidentally shot while shooting grouse. The club went into mourning for over six months, and not a ball was kicked. Some of the players, however, were bitten by the rugby bug and wanted to keep playing even though the club was officially bereaving. One of them, W.Y. Neville, responded to this enforced rest by forming a club in his own village of Felinfoel. That club would go on to provide many players who wore the scarlet shirt, Phil Bennett being the most well known.

Even though the rail network was expanding, it still was not able to offer a huge choice of opposition teams in areas other than the immediate vicinity. Llanelli played clubs based in its own hinterland. The first game played at the club's world famous Stradey was in the 1904/05 season, on 15 October, when they played Swansea.

Of the five games they played in that first season, they lost one and drew four. It wasn't a great start and worse was to come. There was evidence that the game wasn't proving to be such an attraction for the locals. Some called it 'ruffianly', as it obviously offended both Victorian and Welsh Nonconformist sensibilities. Those attitudes stayed around for a while. In 1892, in the *Western Mail* newspaper, a local correspondent by the name of Tinplater mentions that this new game was viewed with considerable misgivings and displeasure. How appropriate that the rugby report was written by a man who took the pseudonym Tinplater. The two were inextricably linked from the blow of that very first whistle.

But, by the time that report was written, the Welsh Rugby Union had already been formed in 1881 at that famous meeting in the Castle Hotel, Neath. The game had spread across south Wales and up north as well, as Bangor were one of the founding clubs. There was no turning back now for this public school game in industrialized south Wales.

By what could be called historical coincidence, the Llanelli team which took to the field against the All Blacks in 1972 played at the end of a long period of industrial history which was the backdrop to the club's formation. It was the club's official centenary year in 1972 also, although the actual date the club began is hotly debated. Two dates are mooted: 1872, as the date a rugby ball was first sighted in the town, and 1875, when the club was officially formed. One could also note 1876 as well, as the date of the first competitive match. The club, with the mighty All Blacks hurtling into town in 1972, obviously favoured adopting the earlier date. However, it can be argued that, without the spontaneous kick-about in one of the town's parks, there would be no subsequent developments which led to the formation of a team. So rugby logic prevailed and 1972 is recorded as the club's official centenary year. The fact they beat the All Blacks in that anniversary year just adds to the whole mythology and rugby folklore. Many of the players on the pitch that October afternoon still believe that '72 was the centenary year and are unaware of any other possibilities, as are the majority of the townsfolk.

Whichever date is actually correct – and does it really matter? – that hundred-year or so period of the club's existence up until the All Blacks game was also a full century of Llanelli industrial might. And that victorious year was at the end of that period of vigour and at the beginning of the decline. The furnaces were not burning quite so brightly, the sun wasn't shining on the black diamonds any more. It was a decade of severe economic decline for Llanelli as its heavy industries folded and were blown away by the winds of economic turmoil. Other areas survived the economic downshift much better than Llanelli did. Duport, the former Klondike, closed its doors in 1981, the last of the steel-making plants. Only Trostre Tinplate Works, which was opened in 1951, still keeps any hint of the heavy industry tradition going, albeit much scaled down and does not have impact on the day-to-day life of the town as it used to. Today Trostre is the name of a thriving retail park, not the centre of tinplate production as it once was. Trostre is more Tesco than tinplate.

Not only was the '72 game at the end of a long chapter of history for the town, but it was also right at the start of a decade which brought the end of traditional values generally. The Seventies were a time of massive change; some would say more long-lasting change than the swinging Sixties. It was the decade when we saw the end of many World War II values, old-fashioned gender values in particular. Revolutionary women's rights acts and equal pay acts were introduced, far reaching even if still insufficient. Industrial unrest was a way of life, with miners' strikes, three-day weeks, no refuse collections and power cuts daily realities. The miners' strike in 1972 was the first one of its kind since the Thirties.

One significant and notable event of the time was a strike held by women who made windscreen wipers. They went on strike for equal pay and were backed by the miners, steelworkers and dockers of Britain in an unprecedented show of strength. The women won what was a landmark victory at the time, with the whole idea of what the term 'working man' was being questioned in a way in which it hadn't in any peace time period.

This was the decade when deference disappeared. The year 1972 was a doorstep to all this change. Not far from Llanelli, not long after the rugby club's famous victory, pioneer punk band, the Sex Pistols, were to declare in a controversial, explosive gig in Caerphilly, that there was 'no future'. Even if you didn't like their music, you knew what they meant. No traditional institution was left untargeted by Rotten and Viscious. Famously, the Queen herself was not immune from being questioned and ridiculed. The pound, the other great symbol of British stability, fell below \$2 for the very first time.

The government had to go cap in hand to the International Monetary Fund. Things were changing.

In Wales, one of our own prophets, film director and playwright Ed Thomas, said in an article in the *Observer* towards the end of the Seventies, that the old Wales was dead, but that the signs of the new Wales were to be seen.

Starting with the Scarlets victory, on the back of the Lions historic Test win in New Zealand in 1971, rugby in the Seventies *wasn't* inextricably linked with the boom of heavy industry. It was, instead, a diversion from the gloom of industrial decline. Luckily, the decade gave us the third golden era of Welsh rugby. It helped revitalise the Welsh world and the world of Llanelli and both had a massive social adrenaline boost on the last day of October 1972. Things would have been a lot darker in Wales and in Llanelli, otherwise.

But, during that first century of Llanelli RFC, for all the tradition of industrial activity, growth and influence, Llanelli town showed one more characteristic which could appear contradictory to all that's been said. It remained a small western town. For all the influx of outside workers and influences, it kept a Welsh identity. Until very recently, it was the largest industrial town where the majority of its people spoke Welsh. The town has held the National Eisteddfod of Wales five times. It was the only industrial town in the world where Welsh was in the majority, as one enthusiastic person wearing Scarlet-tinted glasses once put it. Such a statement shows a strong dose of that not-so-rare commodity, Llanelli bias – a trait never heard on the terraces and in the pubs while discussing the team's performances, of course!

Llanelli is in west Wales, not south Wales. Such a geographical distinction might not exist on maps. But it's a very real psycho-geographical place. Within such an area of consciousness and spirit, Llanelli takes its place at the end of the Valleys, on the edge of the coalfield, just off the end of the motorway. It's Janus looking two ways at once, across to the industrial heartland of the south Wales it's so connected to by blood, sweat and tears. And, in the other direction, to the rural, Welsh-speaking Wales it's connected to by blood, genes and a common tongue. The language divide in Wales is not north-south but east-west.

It can look up to the hills and across the sea just as easily as into the smog. The rolling fields and hills of Carmarthenshire are only an Andy Hill kick away from the town's limits. The sheep haven't all gone, nor the cattle either. The cockles from Penclawdd and laver bread can still be bought on market stalls. For all the innovation, the townspeople are people from the west of their country, with the characteristics of such a geographical condition: the unassuming attitude, the insecurities, the friendliness, the different concept of time, the worldly philosophy that comes from a very simple, in the best sense of the word, way of life and values. To quote the youngest player on the pitch that day in October '72, the unforgettable phrase from the immortal Ray Gravell, 'West is Best' – a saying that comes more from pride than self-confidence. And it's into a town such as this that the touring All Blacks arrived during the last week of October 1972.

Despite the Tinopolises and the Klondikes of the past, one word above all is attached to the town and links the rugby and the heritage together like no other word: Sospan. It can't be saucepan – they didn't make those in Llanelli – they made sospans. Or, if you were a native Welsh speaker, they made sosbans. Not quite in the league of the number of Inuit words for snow, but three spellings for one utensil show its centrality to the mix of the people who made them.

The town's dominant tinplate industry had difficulty meeting the huge demand for tinplate to make kitchen utensils, such as the sospan. The Welsh Tinplate and Metal Stamping Company was opened in the North Docks in 1891. Saucepans dipped in enamel were exported across the world from a factory which employed over 1,000 people. By the 1920s it was the biggest of its kind in Britain: a fitting symbol of the town and the people which created it. Forged in the foundries and exported by enterprise, a simple day-to-day utensil that has a very practical, but essential, use in the family home. And just as there's a huge irony in this public school game being embraced by muscular workers, there's an irony too in this domestic utensil, usually made by women, being seized upon as a symbol of the new macho sporting club in Llanelli. It wasn't long before the town and the rugby team made the song 'Sosban Fach' (Little Saucepan) their own. It will never win any award for the best lyrics anywhere. The tale of Meri Ann having a bad finger, the cat having scratched Little Joni and Dai the soldier's shirt-tail sticking out while the little sospan boils on the fire, isn't exactly the stuff of high poetry. You could be forgiven for thinking that those who penned it had been supporting one of the local businesses, the one in Felinfoel, a little too much!

It comes as no great surprise that many Llanelli people say it was actually composed in the town – doubtless many still think so. As with the rugby club centenary date, why let the facts spoil a good story. They even know where it was written: in the York Hotel, across the way from where that first rugby kick-about happened in People's Park and where the team played its first games. It was opposite one of the town's cinemas, which is now a Wetherspoon's eatery.

But, before settling in Llanelli, the song was much travelled. Copies of this song, not long after the club was formed, exist under the title 'The Llanwrtyd Anthem'. Llanwrtyd is a spa town in mid Wales, many miles from Llanelli. In *Real Llanelli*, Jon Gower elaborates on the Llanwrtyd link. After establishing that the song's origin comes from 'Rules of the Hearth' (1873) composed by Mynyddog, or Richard Davies, Llanbrynmair, he takes the story to Llanwrtyd. 'In 1895 some comic verses were added by Talog Williams, a Dowlais accountant at Llanwrtyd, but one Rev. R.M. Davies also claimed them as his own.'

Despite the geographical distance between Llanelli and Llanwrtyd, the spa town would have been a holiday destination for Llanelli people. But there was also another more direct link with the rugby club. One of the club's early stars was flying winger Percy Lloyd, and he ran a hotel in Llanwrtyd. So, did he bring it to the town when he played there in the 1890s? More than likely.

Add to all that the story of some students at University College of North Wales, Bangor being credited with writing the words, and we have another twist in the tale. But we're not too sure of that either. Following a haphazard journey then, with unanswered questions along the way, the song did settle in Llanelli early on. The notion of a popular folksong that was something to do with sospans and a town which actually produced them, seemed to be a marriage made in heaven, and it's one that's destined to stay together.

One newspaper, *The Cambrian Leader*, refers to it as early as 1896. 'Sospan Fach does seem to have an extraordinary effect upon the Scarlets. The crowd began to sing the ballad of the Little Saucepan... and instantly the old spirit of the Scarlets began to reassert itself and, before the strains had melted away, they were over with what had seemed an impossible try. It was another testimony to the efficacy of the withered finger and Llanelly's splendid pluck.'

We know that by the time of Llanelli's first defeat of a touring side in 1908 – the Walla-Walla-bies which are mentioned in one of the song's verses – the song was recognised worldwide as being Llanelli Rugby Club's. The verse covers the four occasions on which Llanelli have beaten the men from down under, but it was written following the very first victory. After that game, Wallaby forward, Tom Richards – the only man to have played for both Australia and the British Lions, having three caps for each – mentioned in the report of the game in the *Sydney Mail* that 'Sosban Fach' was sung that afternoon. There's no record of him being so pleased that he was part of a game that gave the song a new verse! The Australian team that Llanelli beat went on to play at the London Olympics of 1908, and won the gold medal. The club has long had the distinctive feature of saucepans on the top of their posts.

All the component parts of industry, investment, enterprise, identity and heritage were well established in the town by the time the seventh All Blacks arrived. The pillars were all in place and visible on that grey October afternoon in '72. But they stood in a formation that would probably never be seen again in Llanelli.

3

The waiting game

Rugby may have many problems,
but the greatest is undoubtedly that of the persistence of summer.

Chris Laidlaw, 57 caps for the All Blacks (1963–1970)

AN ALL BLACKS tour to these shores in the 1950s, '60s and into the '70s was a massive national sporting event. Rugby for the New Zealanders has always been all consuming, as Chris Laidlaw's comment above says so succinctly. Another rugby commentator noted that rugby is a religion in New Zealand and only a cult in Britain. That person might not have spent much time in Wales before saying such a thing, but the message about New Zealand is clear enough.

A tour then would shorten that persistent summer, but whenever the All Blacks came to Britain, it wasn't for a holiday. The visit to Britain was hugely anticipated. It was a huge event, easy to underestimate today perhaps, because they are seen on these shores and on television so regularly. And as much as they are still regarded as the definitive rugby side, and the ones to beat, their arrival doesn't carry the same aura, sense of occasion, expectation and thrill as it did those decades long ago.

Their visit to Britain on the 1972/73 tour would have been arranged years in advance. The All Blacks hadn't been so far west since the early 1960s. The captain of the Llanelli team that played them in 1963 was Marlston Morgan. He also played for Llanelli against South Africa in 1960 and Australia in 1967.

By 1972 he had hung up his boots and was on Llanelli RFC's committee.

He had a remarkable career with Llanelli, playing 465 games. And in his case, because there were no substitutes allowed during most of his career – and then only for injury – all the games he played were the full 80 minutes. And, quite often, it was a case of up to 50 games in a season. This is a staggering statistic and difficult to appreciate in this modern era. All done, of course, while keeping a day job down, which in his case was working in the treasury department of the local authority, before then teaching people to drive. He ended up serving on Llanelli's committee for 40 years and he is now president of Llanelli RFC.

Marlston comments, 'There's no doubt that a major emphasis of the committee at that time was making sure that we were always an attractive enough a side to secure a fixture against a touring team. That was the mainstay of the fixture list in any season and it meant doing everything possible both on and off the field to make that happen. In the run up to '72 the main thing we did was separate the administration matters from the rugby itself, a definite change of structure within the club. Carwyn and Norman Gale were both on the committee, but the division of labour changed in the run-up to '72, when they concentrated on more than just rugby matters.'

Celebrating the centenary was a different issue, however. There was no talk of there even being a centenary to celebrate when the conversations about the All Blacks visit first got underway, as former club historian Les Williams recalls. 'The big talk, the build-up, was for the New Zealand game. Then, all of a sudden, somebody mentioned a centenary celebration as well. That was much later on. That decision certainly generated a lot of conversation! Many questioned why 1972 had been chosen as the centenary date. There didn't seem to be a clear answer at the time. But despite some protests, the club stuck with 1972 and a full celebration programme was arranged.'

'After deciding on the centenary year, we were asked to

change the date right up to the beginning of that season,' Marlston Morgan adds. 'But it was too late and we went with '72 as the official date. There's no doubt that a visit from the All Blacks was a deciding factor. We were then asked quite a few times after that season to change the date to the date of the first meeting to form the club officially in 1875. But changing it to one date after celebrating another would have been a silly thing to do.'

So it was decided. It was to be the All Blacks in the centenary season. The forthcoming arrival of the visitors dawned on Llanelli players at different times. They might have all been told at around the same time, but crossing the line from 'knowing' to 'realising' happened at varying stages of each squad member's experience. Their most seasoned player, British Lion and Welsh international Delme Thomas, knew well in advance of 1972 that his home club was facing a big game. 'I knew when we were out in New Zealand with the British and Irish Lions in '71 that Llanelli would be playing against them the following year. I remember Carwyn James, the Lions coach and the Llanelli coach at the time, talking about it towards the end of the Lions tour. That was before we knew we'd won a Test series in New Zealand for the first time. Carwyn would talk to Derek Quinnell and me, as two Llanelli players, and ask us what we thought about playing against the All Blacks for our club back home. That certainly started me thinking, a good 16 months before the All Blacks came to Llanelli. We were right in the thick of a Test series in their country, which made the whole thing more real. Carwyn would love to have a little chat with those of us on the Lions tour who spoke Welsh. He'd come to us most nights – people like Barry John, Gareth Edwards and Gerald Davies – and have a ten, fifteen minute chat in Welsh. The All Blacks coming to Wales cropped up in those chats too and we talked about both Wales and Llanelli playing them.'

Derek Quinnell also recalls those conversations with Carwyn out in New Zealand, saying that it made him start to look forward to playing against a team he had first seen in 1963 as a schoolboy, when his home town took on Wilson Whineray's powerful team. It was the first time many of the '72 squad had seen the All Blacks play, 'I remember Carwyn telling me that I would be facing these guys the following year for my club. He was saying more or less start thinking about that now! It was exciting for me to think that we would be facing an international side again. I had done so in January 1970 against South Africa, when Llanelli very nearly beat them. So I'd had a taste of a big occasion at Llanelli.'

Little did anyone know in the Lions camp in 1971 that by the time the All Blacks came in 1972, 'King' Barry John would have abdicated and hung up his boots for good. The way would have opened up for a successor. It's also, of course, 40 years since he played his last game.

And little did Delme Thomas know, when Carwyn James had those chats with him, that he would be the one to lead his beloved Llanelli out against the mighty All Blacks. Delme didn't play for Llanelli against South Africa in January 1970. Delme wasn't club captain in 1970/71 leading up to the Lions tour. He wasn't captain in 1971/72 after coming home from that tour. He wasn't captain when Llanelli toured South Africa in the summer of '72. But he would be by the time the 1972/73 season kicked off. It's another matter altogether of course whether Carwyn James knew in his own mind who he wanted to be the captain against the All Blacks.

Throughout the 1971/72 season the conversation at Stradey Park and in the pubs and clubs around would no doubt turn to the impending All Blacks visit. Slowly but surely, in the players' minds as well, that chit-chat turned from being eager anticipation to a reality which shaped everything they did on and off the field. Future Wales and Lions star Phil Bennett is one who remembers when the whole focus of their time was defined by two words: 'All' and 'Blacks'. 'As soon as the 1971/72 season finished we were into pre-season training. Carwyn made it clear that we had a big season ahead of us. It was a centenary season, with games organised to mark that occasion and the game against the New Zealanders would be the major focus. "From this day on" Carwyn told us, "we're geared to play against the All Blacks and beat them." Pre-season training was started a little earlier, so that we could prepare properly and thoroughly. Every game, every training session in my mind, was part of the build-up to the last day of October.'

Much has been said about Carwyn James' ability and contribution to the preparations on that day. Many players were also keen to emphasise the contribution of another member of the backroom team, a man who was already working at the club when Carwyn joined in 1969 and who was, at that time, a bit of a rare breed. It's doubtful that any other team in the British Isles had a fitness coach in those days, but Llanelli did.

'Tom Hudson made a huge contribution to Llanelli Rugby Club,' recalls Andy Hill, the winger who scored against the All Blacks. 'He is so underestimated but he changed the way things were done at Stradey in a big way.'

Hudson, then at University College, Swansea, was a pentathlete at the 1956 Olympic Games. He came to Llanelli and completely changed the way players prepared for games. The meeting to bring him to the club was held in the *Western Mail* office in Swansea. The club's then chairman, Peter Rees, was there, as was Glyn Walters, the man behind the microphone at Stradey, who would be editor of the match day programme for the All Blacks game. He worked in that office in Swansea. 'The committee in their wisdom gave us the full blessing to approach him,' says Peter, 'so he was the first official coach of Llanelli RFC and probably the first in Wales. When he came, coaching improved fitness levels along with our execution and pattern of play.'

Peter Rees was the 77th player from Llanelli to be capped for Wales and is the only one left from the Wales team who shared the Championship with England in 1946/47. He was at the helm when another Llanelli innovation was introduced as well, being chairman of the first youth team established by the club in 1964. Four players from that youth team were on the Stradey turf in 1972: Ray Gravell, Hefin Jenkins, Gareth Jenkins and Derek Quinnell. The '72 players were all clear on Tom Hudson's contribution.

Hill continues, 'Most of his emphasis was on pre-season training and conditioning. In my own case, he changed my play completely, improving my fitness, attitude and pace. Two seasons after joining Llanelli, I took up athletics and joined Swansea Harriers, as well as playing for Llanelli.'

A back injury hampered Andy Hill's path to be selected to run for Wales in the Commonwealth Games in 1970, but his speed and skill on the wing meant he scored a phenomenal 312 tries for Llanelli in his career. Llanelli's other wing that October day, J.J. Williams, did represent his country in athletics at those Commonwealth Games.

Tom Hudson introduced new methods to Llanelli, and Phil Bennett remembers one particular fitness trip very well. 'Tom liked to take us to Abercraf, near Neath, to an outdoor pursuits centre there that some say the SAS used for training. I wouldn't be surprised! He'd have us doing these exercises on assault courses, zip glides, the lot. One day, he asked us all to stand facing various trees and to run at them hard as if we were tackling them. We'd never heard of anything like that before! What a sight it must have been on one of those days for two local elderly gentlemen out walking their dogs nearby to see about twenty grown men hugging trees rather too enthusiastically!'

'Tom's approach was certainly more scientific than anything I had seen before,' full back Roger Davies, who had joined Llanelli from Swansea having played for Maesteg as well, remembers. 'I had not seen that kind of approach anywhere else. It was game specific and a lot of training with the ball, which again was new. The main difference could be seen in the last twenty minutes of a game when we could close out the opposition, even if we didn't have the strongest team on the field. We'd also go down to Merthyr Mawr sand dunes with him for a training day in the Welsh athletics camp there. Working out in sand dunes certainly sorted us out, especially when he told us stories of the legendary Australian middle-distance runner, Ron Clarke, training on the same dunes in preparation for the Empire Games in Cardiff in 1958. It didn't go down too well when Tom told us how many more times than us Ron Clarke could run up and down those dunes! That guy set 17 world records during his career and was an Olympic medallist! But that's how Tom pushed us on.'

'And it was commonplace for us to run from Stradey to Burry Port as part of our midweek training, about ten miles there and back probably,' adds second row Delme Thomas 'but when we did that, Tom wouldn't just send us on our way, he would always run with us the whole way.'

Scrum half Selwyn Williams adds, with a cheeky grin, 'Yes we did run to Burry Port and back, but one or two of our number were known, now and again, to jump over the wall of the grammar school down the road from Stradey and hide there while the rest of us went on the run. I won't mention any names, Derek and Shanto!'

By 1972, Tom Hudson was director of physical education at Bath University. In an article in the match day programme on 31 October, he rounds up his thoughts, showing complete confidence in his players. 'Finally, allow me to invite you to watch the closing fifteen minutes of the match with this thought in mind. Llanelli will look fitter and better prepared than their opponents. Maybe the game will be lost but no group of men – particularly at club level – are more dedicated to the cause of their club than these 1972 Scarlets.' Add these thoughts to the forward-thinking philosophy of Carwyn James, and you begin to get a picture of what was happening at Llanelli.

So, change was afoot before the Sixties ended at Llanelli Rugby Club and before Carwyn James arrived. The committee was a progressive one who wanted to see change both on and off the field. The master stroke for the committee, no doubt, was bringing Carwyn James in as the first-team coach. That was at the instigation of former Welsh international, Peter Rees. At the end of the 1960s, rugby brothers Clive and Alan John, brothers of Barry, were playing for Llanelli. They came from the same village as Carwyn James, Cefneithin, and they'd heard that Carwyn was leaving Llandovery College to go to Trinity College, Carmarthen to lecture in Welsh. Peter Rees arranged a meeting with him in Llandovery. 'My wife Nesta and our young son Mark came with me on a Sunday afternoon to Llandovery. We had tea and cakes in the housemaster's room and discussed various things before I made the offer to Carwyn to join Llanelli as coach. He accepted immediately. Eighteen months later he was appointed coach of the British Lions!'

Carwyn was different – a man with an intellectual approach to rugby. The tradition had been, without generalising too much, that rugby teams were looked after by men who were also PE teachers. Llanelli had been led by Tom Hudson and Ieuan Evans before Carwyn, a first step to pushing the coaching boundaries of the late 1960s. Wales' first official coach was Dai Nash in the mid Sixties. Coaching was a relatively new discipline.

The 'thinking' coach approach Carwyn James adopted set out a different way of doing things. In *Scarlet Fever*, the publication which appeared after the victory against the All Blacks in '72, Carwyn notes his gratitude to the committee that backed his ideas. 'May I thank Mr Handel Greville and his committee for leading Great Britain in the matter of selection by asking the coach to be chairman of the selectors and to be responsible for picking his own committee? I immediately accepted and asked Norman Gale to be assistant coach and team manager and invited Delme Thomas as captain to make up a selection committee of three.' He then adds, with typical Carwyn understatement, 'It works well, or at least, I think it does.'

Carwyn says that he was asked, but he had been a committee member for quite a while before the October game and had, according to Marlston Morgan, been making noises about taking the selection responsibilities from the full committee before '72.

It could be said that it would have been difficult for the committee not to allow Carwyn to do as he wished; after all he'd just masterminded the downfall of the All Blacks in their own back yard, but, there were other rugby stalwarts in Wales who'd done exactly that. Having returned as the victorious coach of the '71 Lions, Carwyn had tried for one of the five vice-presidencies of the Welsh Rugby Union. He failed to secure enough votes. We can only begin to imagine how the structure of Welsh rugby might have changed had he been successful. As it was, he had to be satisfied that he was at a club which was leading the way in British rugby.

At the end of that triumphant 1972/73 season, Carwyn James would write in a Welsh rugby magazine about the selection method of rugby teams in general. 'Gone are the days when a full committee of a dozen or more people get together for a couple of hours to select a side. I feel quite strongly in these days of squad systems that selection committees are quite superfluous and I'm sure that you don't need five men to pick the Welsh team.' Clearly, eloquently stated, but spoken in the wrong era. No one was prepared to listen.

But he did have an opportunity to put those words into practice at Llanelli, at least. On arrival, he started work by putting together a squad that would play his brand of expansive rugby – in his own words, 'Rugby football is at its best when the two sides are intent on playing the attacking creative game.' And in the same breath he states that the standard of club rugby in Wales during the 1972/73 season 'wasn't at all high'.

Prior to his arrival there was a tendency at the club, as in most others, to almost have two squads: one for the weekend games and another for the midweek games. Many so-called 'bigger names' didn't want to travel to the far reaches of Upper Cwmscwt on a rainy Wednesday evening. As a result of this, Llanelli would use dozens and dozens of players in one season and they drew on local village teams to plug the gaps left by stay-aways. According to one story, they used a hundred players one season. That did nothing for team cohesion. Tom Hudson had a big part to play in changing this attitude, but Carwyn took it to the next level and developed a squad system. Carwyn James explained his reasoning like this. 'Most leading clubs in Wales are guilty of over-burdening their fixture lists with the result that by the end of an eight-month season players feel a little jaded and stale. For this reason selection committees have to adopt the squad system and rest their key players in some matches to make sure that they have an edge for the important competitive games. In this context, we in Llanelli, and I take full responsibility within the system for this, owe an apology to some clubs for not turning out a full-strength side – one or two of the Monmouthshire clubs have cause for complaint and I sincerely hope that this can be borne in mind in future, otherwise the clubs concerned may lose much of their support.' The future was always on Carwyn James' mind.

The other threat to Welsh rugby in those days, in terms of clubs losing players, came from the other code. Rugby league was played in the north of England. Llanelli lost many top players in the early 1970s. Influential forwards Brian Butler and Stuart Gallagher took the road to the pot of gold up north as soon as the club came back from their summer '72 tour of South Africa; flying wing Roy Mathias also took the same road. Three massive losses. Other players left because they had new jobs that took them out of the area. Some dropped out because of a variety of other reasons. And, of course, a few just weren't picked any more.

In looking at the two games played against touring nations in 1970 and 1972, one thing in particular strikes Derek Quinnell. 'Incredibly, looking at the South Africa game in January 1970 and the All Blacks game in October 1972, within that short space, our side had changed enormously. Only two players played in both games, and that's quite incredible, really. That was me and Hefin Jenkins. Phil Bennett and Delme were around at that time of course, but weren't allowed to play for Llanelli against South Africa because they had been chosen to play for Wales against them that same week. The side that nearly beat South Africa in 1970 was a very young side and you would have thought that it would have stood you in good stead for a long time to come. But that didn't happen. By the time the All Blacks came, we could well have missed the quality and youthful energy of the three who went north between those two games, but Carwyn was building a new squad and was more than aware of what, or who, was needed.'

The only other player who played against South Africa and New Zealand, Hefin Jenkins, is equally surprised at being in such select company, but says that it might not be as random as it appears. 'There were a lot of players who had come through both the youth and schoolboys' system. We all knew each other for a long time before we played in the same first XV. I had known Phil Bennett since I was about 14. Gareth Jenkins and Ray Grav joined the club on the same day. So, although it was only me and Derek who played in both 1970 and 1972, the talent was growing and forming under the surface, as it were. This in addition, of course, to what Carwyn was specifically planning. But it's fair to say that it was predominantly a local team.'

Touring has traditionally been a part of any rugby team's calendar. At the very beginning, Llanelli were one of the first clubs to do so when they toured the north of England. Later on, they were the first club to tour Russia when they visited Moscow in 1957 with a young Carwyn James in their side. There, they reached the final of the world's Youth Festival of Sport. In that year, as well, a new grandstand was opened at Stradey.

For the summer of 1972, a tour had been arranged to South Africa. This was obviously good preparation for meeting the All Blacks later that year. But it was also a difficult choice, as touring South Africa in those apartheid days was fraught with tension and difficulties. Playing South Africa in Llanelli in 1970 was a case in point. Coach Carwyn James was strongly opposed to the discriminatory apartheid system in South Africa at the time. He was not happy that his club were to play a South African team which would be exclusively white; black players weren't even allowed to be considered. He compromised by agreeing to prepare Llanelli for the game, but he refused to watch it, choosing instead to stay in the dressing room as a protest against the attitude shown in the tourists' homeland.

So when it was announced that Llanelli were to tour South Africa, Carwyn James kept to his principles and didn't travel with the team. The tour was coached by Norman Gale.

Before leaving for that tour, it was highlighted that at least one player might have difficulty in obtaining permission to travel to South Africa. It wasn't certain at all if scrum half Selwyn Williams would be given his employer's permission to travel there. 'I was a teacher in Swansea. The local authority didn't want to appear to be backing apartheid in any way by any of their employees having connections with that country. I wrote to the authority to ask for permission to go way before we went, and left it at that.'

This was evidently a situation that Carwyn James was aware of because he started to have conversations with another scrum half in case Selwyn wasn't allowed to go. 'Carwyn knew me from the Lions tour of '71,' says the then Maesteg scrum half, Ray Chico Hopkins. 'He came to talk to me before the end of the 1971/72 season asking me if I wanted to join Llanelli, saying that there was a tour of South Africa coming up and there was uncertainty whether Selwyn was allowed to go or not. Maesteg were playing well at that time and we were heading to win the Championship. So I decided to stay, as tempting as the offer was.'

When the time came to go to South Africa, Selwyn Williams was on the plane. 'I hadn't heard back from the local authority before leaving, and I therefore assumed that meant they weren't going to stop me from going. But when I was out there, one of the boys had a letter from home which included a newspaper cutting. In it was a story about me under a headline which went something like, "Swansea teacher sacked for going to South Africa". I was shocked to say the least. The local authority had refused to give me permission and if I was to go I would be sacked. I was already out there! So I was sacked for the duration of the summer holidays and reinstated at the beginning of the September term, so that the authority could say that no one on their books was in South Africa.'

Once out there, the games were difficult and challenging. Gareth Jenkins recalls that playing in the southern hemisphere was very much a part of the preparation for playing the All Blacks in October. 'It was obvious that that was the case. The type of opposition we would face out there was a good preparation for who we would be facing a few months later. And, as far as we were concerned, as well, the tour was certainly a significant part of a process within the club of developing a squad mentality; they were the early days of a squad system. Traditionally, touring games could throw up all sorts of players we hadn't seen much of before going and would never see after we came back, but this tour included the core of a squad that was being put together deliberately and carefully. That core group stayed together for the best part of ten years.'

In 1972 politics and rugby clashed more than once. Apartheid became the dominant factor in the game in the Seventies. Throughout the world, many rugby players, and sports people in general, had to go through the process of deciding whether or not they'd compete in their sport on South African soil. Some chose to boycott any involvement with a country that segregated people on the basis of their colour. Others chose to argue, quite strongly, that sport and politics didn't mix and therefore there was no reason not to go. Conversely, others argued that keeping the sporting contact was a means of influencing the apartheid regime for the good by forcing an open discussion every time a tour took place. Whichever side they came down on, it was always after much agonising and soul searching. Some players moved from one camp to the other. 'I went with Llanelli to South Africa in '72,' says winger Andy Hill, 'but I refused to go back there with them in 1979. I didn't like what I had seen in '72 at all. Before starting that tour we were given a speech about what we could do and could not do in South Africa. We weren't allowed to chat with the black waiters, to hold the door open for them or acknowledge them in any way. Our hosts would frown on us if we did that. I didn't like it at all and decided not to go back there.'

Llanelli prop Barry Llewelyn turned down the invitation to tour South Africa with the '74 British Lions for the same reason, having already turned down an invitation to go on the '71 Lions tour. But the players didn't judge each other within a team situation for the individual decisions reached. Everyone respected each other's decision, knowing that it hadn't been reached lightly and without cost.

Also that year, the troubles in Northern Ireland spilled into rugby and influenced the field of play. It was the year of the Bloody Sunday massacre when fourteen civil rights protestors were killed by British soldiers in January. The Five Nations competition was due to start in February, but it was not completed for the first time since World War II, as Wales and Scotland refused to play in Ireland.

The event which showed the relationship between sport and politics at its ugliest was the 1972 summer Olympics in Munich. The word 'massacre' was linked to a sporting event. Eleven members and coaches of the Israeli team were killed in a terrorist attack. On three different political fronts, 1972 was a troubled and difficult year for the relationship between sport and politics.

Once the Llanelli team returned home from South Africa and Carwyn was back at the helm, preparations for the All Blacks game intensified. Carwyn still wanted to add to the squad he had carefully crafted since the game against South Africa in 1970. He had three players in mind. Only one of them says that the pending game against the All Blacks was a factor in persuading him to join the men in the west. The other two had other motives in mind. Phil Bennett remembers Carwyn asking him about one type of player he felt he needed specifically. 'Carwyn asked if I knew of a ball carrying back row forward. Round about the same time, I was away with the Crawshays select XV down in the south-west of England. There was a Welsh player there, from Pontypridd, called Tom David. I didn't know him, but on that kind of tour we got to know each other, more off the field than on, as recipients of extremely good Devon hospitality – which at one point, involved a pub full of grown rugby players playing the kids' game Buzz in a drunken stupor late one night, way after closing time! Tom was much better on the pitch than he was playing Buzz after a few too many! I mentioned Tom to Carwyn when I got back – the rugby playing Tom, that is.'

Carwyn was obviously already aware of Tom David through the Llanelli–Pontypridd games. But another encounter with the one Ray Gravell would call 'Tom the Bomb' had stuck in Carwyn's mind. Tom says, 'In the summer of 1971, I had taken time off work with some mates and gone to New Zealand to follow the tail end of the Lions tour. I worked for British Airways then and could fly anywhere in the world for 10 per cent of the normal fare, so out I went. As well as watching some of the games, I went to watch the Lions boys train as well. Carwyn spotted me one day and came over to talk to me, intrigued that I was there to watch them train. This is something he commented on when we met again to discuss me joining Llanelli. It obviously stuck in his mind.'

So, when Phil Bennett mentioned this guy who'd played in the Crawshays team with him, Carwyn already knew who he was talking about. The next step for Carwyn was picking up the phone. 'When the voice on the other end said, "this is Carwyn James", I thought it was a joke to be honest! He wanted to meet for coffee to discuss me joining Llanelli. I said I would gladly meet him but that I was also very happy in Pontypridd. We met, he reiterated his offer for me to join Llanelli, he mentioned the All Blacks game as well, saying that

that was a game I could play in if I kept my form in the games leading up to it.'

Tom David asked for time to think about the offer. But, before Tom got back to him, Carwyn had phoned again, inviting Tom down to see Llanelli play. 'I saw the Barbarians game in September, one of the centenary games. With all the love I have for Pontypridd, I saw straight away that moving to Llanelli would be like moving from Hartlepool to Liverpool in football terms. I asked the advice of some friends and rang Carwyn back the day after to say that I would join.'

Carwyn James held Tom David in high regard. In the year that Carwyn died in an Amsterdam hotel in 1983, Tom David published a book which is as unusual a rugby biography as you're likely to get – with all the respect in the world, it's more like the *Beano* meets an international rugby player with cartoons by Gren! The foreword to the book is an article written by Carwyn when he was sports editor of a weekly newspaper, *Llanelli News*, in the 1970s. In it, Carwyn refers to the Barbarians v New Zealand game at the end of the tour in which Llanelli beat them. He refers specifically to *that* try. 'Vividly I can recall Tom David in the movement set up by Phil Bennett which led to Gareth Edwards' try... In typical Tom David fashion, in went the leading shoulder and with a circular swing of the right arm the ball was delivered safely. With so many other leading flankers, the ball would have gone dead. Amazingly in that movement too, was Derek Quinnell. I say amazingly, because both, although having played superbly, were finding it impossible to get into the Welsh team... Both had been selected on the back of a magnificent display at Stradey on October 31st. Both were feared by the All Blacks and everyone knew it. Everyone it seemed except our national selectors.' No doubt at all then, as to the train of Carwyn's thoughts during those years.

So Tom David was on board. Carwyn invited two other players to go west as well, although both admit that the All Blacks game wasn't such a massive bait for them. After the departure of Roy Mathias up north, there was a gap on the wing. Occasionally, the young Ray Gravell had filled that gap but an out-and-out winger was needed. Carwyn knew where to go and a Bridgend player was in his sights. 'I was well established in Bridgend and had great respect for the club. But I was frustrated that I wasn't getting anywhere on the international front,' explains winger John Williams, or J.J. as he became more popularly known. 'We played Llanelli at the end of the 1971/72 season and they ran us ragged! I remember thinking then that I should have been a part of the team that had played so magnificently. I noticed a weights room there, a medical room and was well impressed because all this was so ahead of its time.'

J.J.'s brother Peter, a former Bridgend player, was by then Maesteg's coach. One evening, J.J. was at his brother's house with scrum half Chico Hopkins. They sat down to watch *Rugby Special* on TV and watched Llanelli play Neath. One thought was now on J.J.'s mind. 'I have to be part of that! Quite simply that was it. It was nothing to do with the All Blacks fixture at all, that wasn't on my mind. My first game was against the Crawshays select XV as part of the centenary celebrations, and then I played against Swansea. I could not believe how massive that fixture was! The passion, the intensity, I loved the big atmosphere! I was also hugely impressed with Carwyn James' thoroughness in preparation and Norman Gale's too. I had a lot of time for Norman as a coach.'

For Carwyn James, filling the other position meant going back to try where he had failed previously. 'Carwyn got back to me then,' says Chico Hopkins, 'and asked me again to join Llanelli. A lot went through my mind, well it would when someone like Carwyn comes calling the second time! We had failed to secure the Championship at Maesteg at the end of 1971/72 season by a whisker. Some of their leading players were retiring, about five of them. So my thinking was that if we failed with those five, what chance would we stand in the following season without them? Also, I thought about my own situation. If Maesteg were not to do so well, where would that leave my international prospects? I would quite likely be ignored.'

Chico Hopkins had earned his one cap in a memorable game against England in 1970. With 25 minutes left and Wales trailing, Gareth Edwards was injured and had to come off. Chico took his place and scored the try which gave Wales a memorable victory. From then on he was seen as Gareth Edwards' understudy and went on to be chosen for the Lions tour of '71, where again he came on for Gareth in a Test and played exceptionally well.

'My thinking by the time of Carwyn's second call was simple. If I moved to Llanelli I would be with a bigger club, my international chances, challenging Gareth Edwards, would be far greater with them. And a huge bonus would be teaming up with Phil Bennett as outside half, who was trying to prove himself as an international in that position too. There was no big decision really and I went west!'

None of the three new players were at the club when Llanelli played their first game of the centenary season. That was an encounter with the London Welsh exiles. They had agreed to kick off the centenary celebrations despite the fact that they'd just returned from a tour of the Far East, either on the day of the match or the night before, depending on whose account you believe! They certainly did go straight from the airport down to Llanelli. Phil Bennett remembers it well. 'I remember John Dawes coming up to me and asking us to take things easy with them because they had just come back from a long tour, and that the game was a centenary celebration game as well. I said OK, no problem, we'll play gently. But at the same time, Delme, as captain, had been firing up the players unaware of my chat with John, saying that this game was part of our preparation to face the All Blacks, so there could be no slacking. Our two centres, Grav and Roy Bergiers, absolutely hammered their back line and went in to everything with 150 per cent commitment. John turned to me during the game and said, with a pleading voice, "Phil, what happened to taking it easy? You're taking us apart!" I told him not to worry and that there would be an extra gin and tonic in it for him after the game. We went on to beat them 31–0!'

So the 'official' centenary season had arrived. Many events were organised, including a Gymanfa Ganu, a hymn-singing festival, which was filmed by HTV. There was a festive air in the town. A centenary is something that brings people together, especially in a rugby town. It gave an injection of social pride. But the team to play against the All Blacks had still not been selected. That was the next step.

4

The selecting game

I wanted [to write] a play that would paint the full face of
sensuality, rebellion and revivalism. In south Wales, these
three phenomenon have played second fiddle only to rugby,
which is an amalgamation of all three.

Gwyn Thomas, Welsh author and playwright

THE ALL BLACKS game was looming ever larger with only
weeks to go. The time came to choose the team to play against
them. The selection group that Carwyn had been allowed to
put together to prepare for the game: Norman Gale, Delme
Thomas and himself, met to decide who would be playing.

'We met at Carwyn's house in Cefneithin,' Delme Thomas
recalls, 'and the whole discussion was over in about an hour. It
was fairly straightforward. That is, apart from three positions.
There was a little talk about the full back position, with
Bernard Thomas' name mentioned. But that wasn't too serious
a suggestion, more mentioned in passing. Roger Davies was
the obvious first choice for us all. But the other two were a
little bit more difficult. Alan James and Selwyn Williams had
been faithful servants to Llanelli and it was very difficult for me
personally to even discuss the possibility of them not playing.
Don't get me wrong, it wasn't a case of having any problem with
Tom David or Chico Hopkins; they were obviously talented
players. But I felt bad that we were talking of Alan and Selwyn
maybe not playing.'

After the three had their meeting, Phil Bennett was invited

to join them, in a sort of vice-captain capacity. He was captain of the team's tour to South Africa the previous summer. No sooner had he arrived in Cefneithin than Carwyn said they were on their way out for a meal. 'That was typical of Carwyn,' Phil Bennett says, 'he loved eating out. So, the four of us went up to the Angel in Salem, near Llandeilo. We talked and talked about the game, the team and the whole occasion. But I had no input into the selection; it was obvious that had been done in Carwyn's house, and rightly so.'

Carwyn James later summed up how he felt about that selection process. 'In a town like Llanelli where the commitment is so overwhelming, where scores of people turn up to watch our training sessions, where hardly anything but rugger is discussed at work, one realised what a responsibility it was. I must confess that I lost sleep before the selection of the team to play the All Blacks... but all in all I don't think I would have it otherwise... Norman, Delme and I have had our problems, but usually it was a case of who to leave out, such is the wealth of talent available.'

That wealth of talent played against London Welsh ten days before 31 October, in London. They were well beaten. Carwyn had negotiated a ten-day break for the club in the fixture list, so that they could prepare without the demands of league rugby. 'I wanted that gap so that if someone had an injury there would be time to recover. Of course, I can get the team on the boil then too. We have had a very difficult September and October and have played most of the top clubs. During the ten days, the side can regain any of the edge they may have lost.'

After the London Welsh game, it turned out that there was another benefit to the gap negotiated by Carwyn. 'That defeat was the best thing that could have happened to us probably,' states Delme Thomas. 'We knew that there was no way we could beat anybody playing like we did in London. We needed to be sorted out and, by making sure we didn't have a game after that before the All Blacks, Carwyn had time to work with us. Lucky he did. He spent the time training us, night after night, working on the weaknesses shown against London Welsh.'

As well as playing against teams such as London Welsh (who had no shortage of British and Irish Lions in their midst), and both the Crawshays and Barbarian select XVs as well as the South African opposition on tour, there was another crucial element to the way Llanelli prepared. Again, it involved another Carwyn innovation, according to Delme. 'During midweek training one week, Carwyn had arranged for some of the local village teams to come in and play against us. That meant that we had a full match against a full team as our training. Kidwelly, Tumble, New Dock Stars and other village teams were all brought in over a period of weeks. That was so different for us!'

Gareth Jenkins agrees that playing these teams was an invaluable move. But he also adds that while Carwyn had the vision, it was his assistant Norman Gale who delivered it. Delme Thomas sums up that vision with his usual humility and graciousness. 'There's no doubt that those village teams, every one of them, and every player who played for them against us, had their part to play in the victory our team had on 31 October. They owned part of that victory too.'

One particularly gruelling training method has stuck in prop Barry Llewelyn's mind. It involved the popular Tanner Bank on the north side of the Stradey pitch. This was where the vocal fans gathered and where the banter was at its best. It was originally built – if that's the word for a terraced bank – from the rubble of defunct World War II air-raid shelters from the surrounding area. It was opened officially in September 1953, before Llanelli played the All Blacks a month later. By the 1970s the Tanner Bank was covered by concrete steps and occasional rails. But not all the way according to Barry. 'If you were facing the Tanner Bank, to the left, there was a bank of gravel, ash and rubble where nobody usually stood to watch games. Either Carwyn or Norman had the bright idea of using that area for training. So the pack were taken there and got into scrum formation at the foot of the bank. Another pack was called to pack against us – but they were higher up the slope of the bank than us and, on top of that, they had two extra players. So the first-team pack had to stand at the bottom of a rubble bank and push uphill against a pack of ten! Gruelling! But effective in the end!'

So, the inner circle knew who the team was, but they hadn't made their announcement. Carwyn had one more trick up his sleeve in the plan which he'd been slowly unveiling for the best part of two years. After that selection meeting, and further discussions with Phil Bennett, Carwyn took the whole squad to see the All Blacks' first game of their tour, against Western Counties in Gloucester. That was on the Saturday before they would face the New Zealanders. Taking the whole squad to see the opposition play someone else was certainly not the done thing in those days and it was regarded as rather a novelty.

Some couldn't go to Gloucester due to injury, Phil Bennett being one of them. 'I was carrying a shoulder injury at the time and I didn't think that a trip to Gloucester would do it any good,' recalls the number 10. 'I had been told that I needed to do some exercises to strengthen it. So the thought of hours in a coach to the West Country, followed by a few hours standing in the cold watching a game, then back home again, didn't fill me with excitement. I was advised that it would be better to stay home and make sure I played. That made sense to me!'

But all the Llanelli players who were able to go to Gloucester came away with almost an identical impression. Chico Hopkins remembers that they had to stand to watch the whole match, in one corner of the enclosure, with no special treatment. Gareth Jenkins, seeing the All Blacks live for the very first time, was impressed by their size, physicality and the brutality of the rucking. 'We all knew that if we didn't have the guts to get in there, to be hurt, they would overwhelm us as they did Western Counties.' He adds, 'Their psychological intimidation was obvious too and we knew we had to deal with that. We had to be brave enough to take the shoeing, we just had to be. We could in no way be intimidated or that would be it.'

English international and future British Lion, Mike Burton, played for Western Counties, recalls Derek Quinnell. 'He still tells me today that what they did that day was soften the All Blacks up for us!'

There was no doubt in the mind of every player who went to Gloucester that they could beat the All Blacks. Carwyn James was of the same mind. When they returned to Llanelli, Phil Bennett went to meet them and was overwhelmed by the sense of confidence in his fellow players.

The team was announced on the Sunday after the Gloucester game. That is, if the consensus rule is applied. Not all the players can remember when the team was announced, but just over half go for that Sunday, two days before the game. But, television footage shows Carwyn addressing the squad and saying that he'd met with Norman and Delme the night before to select the team. So it couldn't have been that Sunday after all, as they were on their way back from Gloucester the night before. The players knew then, when they travelled to Gloucester who was playing and who wasn't. There were no major surprises, only one or two – the two that Delme was painfully aware of on the day of selection at Carwyn's house.

For Delme, the loyal club man, that made things very difficult as it meant leaving long-standing team mates on the bench. If Carwyn lost some sleep back then, Delme is still not at ease to this day about some of the choices made. It still causes some heart wrenching for him. Indeed, many of the players share his feeling that the one player most hard done by through not being selected was Selwyn Williams. Delme still feels he let two fellow players down. 'I suppose if I'm honest, I think that Selwyn should definitely have played even though, as it turned out, Chico had a great game on the day.'

'I knew as soon as Chico joined us that things weren't looking good,' Selwyn Williams recalls today. 'I couldn't feel the same from that moment on about the All Blacks game. When I joined the Scarlets, I was used at first as the Wednesday night scrum half, with Gareth Thomas being used on the Saturday afternoons. I got my chance in the game against South Africa because Gareth was injured and I came on as a sub in the second half. But after that I had established myself as the main number 9. I wasn't picked for the game against London Welsh ten days before, and I knew then that things weren't looking good. My reaction to the All Blacks game changed after that. I got the definite impression that Carwyn made the decision for the good of the team obviously, but that it was a difficult decision for him. The reason I say that is the way he reacted to me after making the decision, which was always making sure I was OK.'

'In a strange way, I could totally understand how Selwyn felt, because I was in the same predicament as him with Wales. I felt that I should have been chosen so many times instead of Gareth Edwards,' says Chico, 'and I was on the bench way over twenty times for Wales. I really did understand, and I still do. The two of us were going for one position.'

Today, Selwyn Williams is still philosophical about that selection issue. There is, however, one thing that has made it more difficult for him over the years since the game. 'When the conversation comes round to the fact that I played rugby for Llanelli in the 1970s, people invariably say, "Oh! You must have played against the All Blacks then!" And to have to say, "Well, actually no I didn't" isn't easy, if I'm honest.'

I put it to him that under today's substitution system, he certainly would have played a part in the game, even if he came on during injury time. His answer is equally honest, 'I probably would have preferred that to be the case. Because then, when people say that I must have played against the All Blacks, I could have at least said yes. And then gone on to explain I came on as sub for however many minutes. But the first reply would be a yes and that would have made all the difference.'

Such dilemmas, of course, are the stuff of rugby and other team sports. Many of the individuals involved in that game were no strangers to being on the wrong end of selection decisions. Chico has already explained his own frustrations. Carwyn James himself knew all about being kept out of the Wales team, as the great Cliff Morgan limited his caps tally to just two. Llanelli back row forwards Hefin Jenkins and Gareth Jenkins were kept out of the Wales set-up by Merv 'the Swerve' Davies and John Taylor respectively. And the ever-popular Roy 'Shanto' Thomas, the Scarlets hooker, must surely have some sort of record for being on the subs bench 25 times for Wales without ever getting a cap. If he was playing today, he probably would have had 25 caps, even if he came on during injury time only. He would be on the receiving end of plenty of dressing room banter at Stradey for that fact, with comments such as, 'Why do you bother going to Cardiff at all Shanto; all you do there is nurse splinters in your backside!'

Once the '72 season had started, the centenary celebrations and the build-up to the All Blacks game soon mingled into one. Officially, the game against the Barbarians, on 27 September, was a centenary game, but provided ideal opposition to the Llanelli side a few weeks before the All Blacks. Whatever happened on the pitch (Llanelli won 33–17), the game gave the rugby world one of those Tanner Bank banter gems.

With things not going too well for the home team, Barbarian players were deemed not to be in the spirit of things according to the Scarlet faithful. One clear voice was carried by the wind from the Tanner Bank towards some of the Barbarian players on the pitch, 'Go back to Barbaria...!' was the shout. This was noted by none other than former rugby star Clem Thomas in his column in the *Observer*, as well as by other rugby pundits, official or otherwise.

The scoreboard at Stradey was different to what the All Blacks were used to, even in Wales – it needed to be prepared differently for the All Blacks visitors. Since Carwyn's arrival at the club, the scoreboard always carried the name of the opposing team in Welsh. That had begun a while before the '72 season. The scoreboard remained in Welsh until Stradey closed its gates for the last time. Some have said that it was Grav's innovation. But in this case, that can't actually be true, as in '72 he was the youngest player in the team, with little influence. That was to come later. When he was president, he did have a say in the introduction of a Dafydd Iwan song, 'Yma o Hyd', as the music to be played when the team scored. This was instigated when the second youngest player on the field in October '72, Gareth Jenkins, became Llanelli coach in the 1990s. Gareth Jenkins was a day older than Grav.

Twenty years ago, following another famous victory when Llanelli beat the then world champions Australia, that same scoreboard was still in Welsh. Llanelli on top and Awstralia underneath. On handing back to the *Grandstand* studio after the game, presenter Steve Rider congratulated the Scarlets on a memorable victory, but had to add something like '... shame they couldn't get the spelling right on the scoreboard!' This prompted a host of Welsh fans to phone the BBC to complain, and the usually smooth, unflappable Mr Rider had to apologise on air for insulting the Welsh!

The town itself also got ready for the All Blacks visit in '72. There were floral displays of all kinds, including an official one within the grounds of the town hall to mark the centenary. The town's shops held a competition for the best window display, which was sponsored by the *Western Mail*, the national newspaper of Wales. Before the day of the game, the interest and support for the Llanelli–All Blacks fixture extended much further than the usual Llanelli catchment area, and the town centre was a hub of excitement.

But it wasn't all plain sailing even back in the town. In the *Llanelli Star* on the Saturday before the All Blacks game, there was one story of huge disappointment to the fans. One of the town's pubs had some bad news. This is how the *Star* tells the story: 'There will be no drinking pints in the Clarence Hotel during Tuesday's All Blacks match. Licensee of the Murray Street pub, Mr Ronald Crome, applied to Llanelli magistrates on Thursday for an extension between 3 p.m. and 5 p.m. "I've had a number of customers who wish to watch the second half of the All Blacks game on our colour TV," he said. "A number of people had failed to get tickets," he added. Inspector William Robert Lawrence said the police objected to the application. "The majority who are interested in rugby have obtained tickets," he said. But people could be allowed on the premises without it being licensed.' The magistrates rejected the application. It's not clear if anyone took up the option of being in the Clarence without a drop of alcohol being served. If it did happen, it was undoubtedly a rugby first!

The team's preparations also suffered a setback that Carwyn James wasn't happy with at all. Four Llanelli players had been chosen to go to Murrayfield to play in a game between Wales/England and Scotland/Ireland. Phil Bennett was chosen to start and Chico Hopkins, Roy Bergiers and Derek Quinnell were travelling reserves. Carwyn thought that this was a heavy toll for one club to bear and referred to it as 'a bit rough'. He rationalised it in this way. 'The selectors must think they are the best men in England and Wales. It is a tribute to the club, but this and the calls on the side for the Wales B international has ruined two matches for us. Our preparation for the All Blacks match at the end of the month has gone by the board as far as match practice is concerned.'

There were also injuries to deal with. As well as Phil Bennett, Gareth Jenkins, the young flanker, also suffered an injury in the weeks leading up to the game. He'd done something to his groin. This overshadowed everything else at the time. 'I had no great expectation that I would be playing against the All Blacks anyway, to be honest. I was young, inexperienced and with no guarantee in my mind that I would play. An injury in mid September seemed to make that more certain. But, Carwyn decided that I needed serious treatment for my groin and sent me to Harley Street! He'd arranged for me to be in London for two weeks in order to receive the best treatment. My mother lived in London and I was able to stay with her while I was there. Ever thinking everything through properly,

Carwyn had also arranged for me to train with Harlequins while I was up there. So it was two weeks of living with my mum, having intense physiotherapy and injections in Harley Street and training with the Harlequins! That's how I prepared for the All Blacks game!'

With his treatment over, Gareth came back and played the one game before facing the All Blacks – back in London against London Welsh, the one they lost badly. But he was selected and would face the All Blacks ten days later.

Throughout the town and the surrounding villages, thousands of fans: men, women and children were gearing up for the game, waiting for those tickets to arrive in the post, arranging time off, studying the form and bragging about the Llanelli boys over a pint. The local newspaper played its part in the hype. The Saturday before the game, it was unequivocal: 'Llanelli's hopes lie with these men. If they beat the All Blacks, their names will be immortalised.' It was pressure and expectation of an almost religious intensity.

5

The All Black game

You can go to the end of time, the last World Cup in the history of
mankind, and the All Blacks will still be favourites for it.

Phil Kearns, member of two World Cup winning Australian teams

SO WHERE DID it all begin, this regular cross-hemisphere
warfare that brings the All Blacks to these shores with such
huge expectation? What are the origins of the tradition which
established them as the ones to beat? And why do Wales feel so
close to the All Blacks? The All Blacks' air of invincibility has
been around for a very long time. They feel it themselves too,
as their motto is 'Subdue and Penetrate'. They've been coming
to these shores for well over a hundred years now, and who can
forget that very first visit.

Neither the Welsh nor the All Blacks have erased that game
from their collective sporting memory, albeit for entirely
different reasons. For the record, Wales won due to a hotly
disputed disallowed try. The All Blacks exciting centre, Deans,
claims to have grounded the ball over the try line. The referee
didn't allow it however, as Deans claims a Welsh player, scrum
half Owens, had picked the ball up and placed it just short of
the line, which is where the ref saw it by the time he caught
up with the play. Oh, for a TMO to sort it out! That was ten
minutes before the end of the game and Wales won 3–0.

There's nothing like a controversial win to set the tone for
the following decades. The relationship between the two rugby
nations was firmly established on that day in 1905.

The game was significant in so many ways. The was-it-a-try-or-not dispute only added to what was already a fully charged occasion. Understanding that 'charge' explains the course of Wales–All Blacks occasions from then until now. The man who writes so eloquently about both the history of Wales and Welsh rugby, Professor Dai Smith, says that for all that's happened since 1905 between the two countries, nothing has happened 'that was not prefigured in 1905 when Wales first faced New Zealand on the rugby field.' He goes on to say, 'They clashed as two superb teams, both conquerors of all that was in sight; the aura of mutual invincibility was a major factor in the making of this epic encounter.'

Wales were, quite simply, superb in the years leading up to 1905. They had won the Triple Crown in 1893 and 1904, and would claim another five Crowns before 1911. They had not been beaten at home since 1899. This was the first golden era of not only Welsh rugby, but rugby itself.

The All Blacks, for their part, were on a 36-match tour, 32 of those games in the British Isles, one in France, one in New York and two in Canada. Their game against Wales was number 28 on the list. They had won every one of their previous 27 matches and would win the eight matches after the Welsh game too. They scored 1,022 points and conceded only 72!

The All Blacks management knew before leaving home that Wales would be their stiffest test, due to the way they played the game on the field. But there were other considerations too. New Zealanders wanted to do well in England because it was, after all, the mother country. They were the colonists. They wanted to show that they had come of age, that they were, in fact, different, separate. Which brings us back once again to rugby and a nation's identity.

When they came to Wales, just over a week before Christmas 1905, they realised that they were somewhere they'd never been before – and not just geographically. The All Blacks party testify to not having encountered an atmosphere like the one they experienced in Cardiff that day in any of their previous matches. The New Zealand captain, David Gallaher, put it very simply, 'We never had such a reception anywhere.'

In their encyclopaedic book, *A Century of All Blacks in Britain and Ireland*, Fox, Bogle and Hoskins quote a journalist's account of the pre-match atmosphere. According to J.A. Buttery, Cardiff was 'a continuous crackle of ardent Celtic chatter, broken every now and again by the deep harmonious resonance of some patriotic refrain.'

The *South Wales Daily News* takes the language and the references even further. 'Public enthusiasm was as fervent as on the morning of some great Waterloo when the destinies of Empires hung in the balance.' It goes on to say that 'Cardiff, on that day, was the epicentre of the old world and the new; that patch of grass the battleground for two nations, not two rugby teams. There was the old world, the new world, and there was Wales.'

In the run-up to the game, there had been much talk in pubs and debate in the press as to why these New Zealanders were so good. The general consensus was that it was due to the genes they'd all taken with them from the British Isles in the first place. Those genes had had a better climate to develop fully in the southern hemisphere. Whatever the real genetic reason, press reports of games before they got to Wales were all saying much the same. Words such as 'quicker', more 'initiative', 'better men physically' and 'greater resolution' were used to describe them. And even though Wales knew well in advance of 1905 that the All Blacks were on their way, they did not begin to prepare seriously for the game until they started to hear these reports of how magnificently the All Blacks had played on the tour already.

Ironically, one decision made to help preparations in light of realising how good the All Blacks actually were, was to take the Welsh team to see the All Blacks play. They all went to see the team play Gloucester at Kingsholm (the same ground to which Carwyn James took his Llanelli team in 1972). The 1905 Wales team would have seen the All Blacks tear Gloucester apart, 44–0. They also defeated Yorkshire 40–0 the week before they came to Wales. They had beaten England, Ireland and Scotland and the Wales match was given the over the top label of a world championship decider. Subsequently, as Bill O'Keefe and Emyr Young say in their book, *The Arms Park: Heart of a Rugby Nation*, 'Public anticipation was whipped up to fever pitch by a hysterical press.'

The Wales–All Blacks game of 1905 was not an all-ticket match. Tens of special trains were laid on to bring fans to Cardiff from all directions. The docks closed early, so that the dockers could be at the match. The streets from the railway station to the Queen's Hotel, the All Blacks HQ, were so full, the brakes carrying the team were down to walking pace for most of the journey. Dai Smith quotes from the diary of George Dixon, the All Blacks manager, 'It was somewhat embarrassing and certainly a novel experience to the Maori participants in such a royal progress... the greeting to Wales will live long in the memory of every member of the team.'

There was controversy before the teams reached the pitch. George Dixon refused the list of four suggested referees for the match. The Welsh Union had submitted the list as required, but George wasn't happy. In the end, they settled on a Scotsman, John Dallas, an inexperienced referee who was younger than both captains that day.

One piece of history made that day too was seeing the famous haka in Wales for the first time. The *Western Mail* described it as 'not very musical but very impressive'. Wales had a trick up their sleeve too and had a plan to counter the haka's effect. It had been suggested during the week before the game that the Welsh should sing their national anthem. At least, the hope was that enough would know the chorus in order to join in when it was played by the Welsh Regiment's Second Battalion Band. 'Hen Wlad fy Nhadau' was fifth on the list of songs they planned to play before the game anyway. The plan was executed, and the Welsh anthem was sung heartily after the All Blacks' intimidating haka, the first time the national anthem was sung before a game. It certainly made an impression on a journalist writing for a New Zealand newspaper. He talks of the fervour of the Celtic heart, and it being the most impressive incident he has ever witnessed at a game. He adds, 'It gave a semi-religious solemnity to this memorable contest... intensely thrilling, even awe-inspiring.' We too have an intimidating musical weapon in our national anthem.

'Our national anthem,' says former Wales First Minister, Rhodri Morgan, 'makes this strange transition from its words of praise for the loss of blood of slain heroes of the battlefield, into encouragement of heroic effort on the sports field. It is sung, not to the marching rhythms of most national anthems, but to a waltz tune composed in the backroom of a pub in Pontypridd by the local pub harpist. That's Wales for you in a nutshell!'

One English author, journalist and MP, J.P.W. Mallalieu, who was MP for Huddersfield from 1945 to 1979, was fully aware of the impact and significance of the Welsh anthem being sung at rugby games. 'The Welsh crowd will sing 'Land of My Fathers' against Ireland, Scotland and against France. But it sings best against England, for, against England, there are old scores to be paid off, scores which were notched against My Fathers long before rugby was first played.'

Despite all the enthusiasm and obvious passion that day in 1905, rugby in Wales was still not universally accepted. The opposition previously mentioned had not all gone away. There was also another new contributory factor. The above journalist's reference to semi-religious atmosphere could not have been more appropriate. The year 1905 was the end of a period of religious revival in Wales, which saw tens of thousands of people turn to God. This did have a big effect on rugby. The captain's board at many clubhouses throughout Wales shows a gap during the years 1904/05, when all rugby was suspended as players went to chapel and prayer meetings instead. In some cases, rugby posts were cut down.

But not all those who objected to rugby shaped their view

on revivalist principles, however. O'Keefe and Young quote a very famous Welshman in this context. In 1895, David Lloyd George complained that 'morbid footballism' was distracting Welsh attention from more serious matters. He was converted however, and in 1907 he visited the Arms Park to watch Cardiff play and declared afterwards, 'It is a most extraordinary game. I never saw it before and I must say I think it is more exciting than politics.' It's interesting that his 1895 comments were made without him ever seeing a game! Nearly 40 years after rugby clubs had been established in Wales, it was still drawing people to see the game for the first time and still having to persuade people of its appeal. There's no doubt that the 1905 game played a huge part in that. The fact that the opposition was New Zealand cemented yet another early layer of Welsh rugby heritage.

After the victory, journalists and editors were suitably inspired to write the most glowing prose in praise of the Welsh heroes. The *South Wales Daily News* will suffice as an example. In comparing the size of Wales to other nations, and the fewer opportunities to show off both mental and physical powers, the editor harks back even further to explain just what had happened that day. 'The great quality of defence and attack in the Welsh race is to be traced to the training of the early period when powerful enemies drove them to their mountain fortresses. There was developed then, those traits of character that find fruition today.'

The fans just enjoyed the ecstasy of the moment and ran to the pubs of Cardiff, which almost all had to lock their doors within fifteen minutes of the end of the match. It would take until 1972 for pubs to be drunk dry in another victory celebration!

This is how the New Zealand Rugby Union's own official history sums up the 1905 game. 'In the United Kingdom especially, the team's largely confident, attractive and comfortable wins made a strong statement about the quality of rugby in the colonies and New Zealand in particular. Moreover, the 1905–06 tour gave rise to the famous "All Blacks" moniker, as the fame surrounding the black-clad team spread. Nowadays, this team is known as the Originals – they were the first team to demonstrate the power and skill of New Zealand rugby, the first to make rugby a part of New Zealand's cultural identity, and the first to be known as All Blacks. It is also thought that this saw the emergence of the Kiwi as a national symbol.'

The year 1905 was then the beginning of so much. But it's also worth stepping aside for a moment to look at what was there before that seminal year. Much is made of the impulsive decision by William Webb Ellis to pick up the ball and give birth to the game of rugby. But there were examples in many countries of native games which could be called early 'relatives' of the game. That's why the Webb Ellis story was mentioned rather sceptically previously. On opposite ends of the earth, New Zealand and Wales were no exception.

Both nations had indigenous ball games that existed before rugby was thought of. In Wales it was called cnapan. In New Zealand it was called ki-o-Rahi. Both are said to have influenced the game of rugby that developed in each country. They certainly fed the raw instincts that found a later, natural competitive and sporting expression on rugby fields. It has been suggested that ki-o-Rahi may have influenced New Zealand playing styles.

Ki-o-Rahi is a fast-paced game, played with a small round ball called a 'ki'. It is especially popular in Maori communities. Two teams of seven players play on a circular field divided into zones, and score points by touching the 'pou', which are the boundary markers, and by hitting the 'tupu' or target. It has a lot in common with rugby and Australian Rules football. It is still massively popular. All Blacks legend Wayne Shelford has represented his country at both rugby and ki-o-Rahi, the first double international. He played 22 Tests for the All Blacks and captained New Zealand in a ki-o-Rahi international against France in 2010. The indigenous Welsh game doesn't sound as organised or as structured as the New Zealand one. Called cnapan, it was played until the end of the nineteenth century, mainly in west Wales.

The game was described in detail as far back as 1604! This is what George Owen said about cnapan then:

> The ancient Britons being naturally a warlike nation did no doubt for the exercise of their youth in time of peace and to avoid idleness devise games of activity where each man might show his natural prowess and agility... and surely for the exercise of the parts aforesaid this cnapan was prudently invented. For in it, beside the exercise of the bodily strength, it is not without resemblance of warlike providence... About one or two of the clock afternoon begins the play, in this sort, after a cry made both parties draw to into some plain, all first stripped bare saving a light pair of breeches, bare-headed, bare-bodied, bare legs and feet... for if he leave but his shirt on his back in the fury of the game, it is most commonly torn to pieces and I have also seen some long-lock gallants, trimly trimmed at this game not by clipping but by pulling their hair and beards.
>
> The foot company thus meeting, there is a round ball prepared of a reasonable quantity so as a man may hold it in his hand and no more, this ball is of some massy wood as box, yew, crab or holly tree and should be boiled in tallow for make it slippery and hard to hold. This ball is called cnapan and is by one of the company hurling bolt upright into the air, and at the fall he that catches it hurls it towards the country he plays for, for goal or appointed place there is none neither needs any, for the play is not given over until the cnapan be so far carried that there is no hope to return it back that night, for the carrying of it a mile or two miles from the first place is no losing of the honour so it be still followed by the company and the play still maintained, it is oftentimes seen the chase to follow two miles and more... It is a strange sight to see a thousand or fifteen hundred naked men to concur together in a cluster in following the same which is hurled backward and forward...

The language might be over 400 years old, but it describes some scenes which were not a million miles away from those seen at rugby grounds the world over every week! Imagine over a thousand men playing with a small ball over more than a mile between villages. The first rugby teams started to be formed at the end of the nineteenth century and remnants of the cnapan game were still played in some areas in west Wales. At the time the press were concerned about the ruffian element of rugby – they obviously hadn't gone far enough west and seen cnapan played!

Both New Zealand and Wales could recall ancient games which rugby would later replace. Both could draw on a far older sporting heritage. As author Gwyn Thomas said, 'Rugby as played by the Welsh is not a game. It is a tribal mystery.' That tribal mystery goes back a long way.

As in Wales, rugby's first connection with New Zealand was through the upper classes – the colonial public school influences. Indeed, at first, rugby was seen as a way that the New Zealanders could show their loyalty to the British Crown. The game was taken there in 1870 by a former pupil of Christ's College, Finchley, who was the son of the Speaker of the New Zealand House of Representatives. Two other former pupils of that Finchley College made significant and long-lasting contributions to world rugby too. Shepstone Giddy is credited with introducing rugby to South Africa and W.P. Carpmael founded the Barbarians rugby tradition. Further proof, if it were needed, that rugby's genesis and subsequent exodus throughout the world was very much as a result of the public school system.

It was the New Zealand Natives rugby tour of 1888/89 which showed that New Zealand could compete with other nations. There had been various forms of rugby on the islands from the early 1860s, with Christchurch Club formed in 1863. But the first rugby match, as we know it, to be played in New Zealand, took place in Nelson in May 1870, between Nelson College and Nelson Football Club. This was a full two years before John Rogers took the game to Llanelli for the first time.

One hundred years after that first rugby match, a New

Zealander whose father was Samoan and his mother a Rarotongan of Samoan descent, earned his first cap for the All Blacks. Bryan Williams would go on to distinguish himself as a superb winger, making his first mark on his country's tour of South Africa in 1970. He was, quite simply, a sensation, scoring 14 tries in his 13 appearances, scoring in each of the first and fourth Tests. He had his own dispute as a result of the apartheid situation on that tour. In order to have permission to go, he had to obtain official honorary white status because of his mixed race background. Once on the tour, he had a hard time from the white spectators. Two years later he came to Stradey Park to face Llanelli, having scored three tries against Western Counties at Gloucester.

The seventh All Blacks left their hotel in Cheltenham the morning after conquering the Western Counties. The All Blacks made Swansea their base from Sunday until the Tuesday morning of the game. They stayed at the Dragon Hotel, the area's premier hotel and were looked after by members of Swansea RFC. One of the journalists travelling with them refers to the hospitality they received as getting better and warmer the further west they went.

During an interview for this book, from New Zealand's team hotel in Buenos Aires on their Argentinian tour, Bryan Williams, now president of his country's rugby union, emphasises that 1905 is still part of the All Black consciousness. 'It certainly is. We grow up in New Zealand as rugby players understanding 1905 and its significance. I go in to teach at an academy in Auckland and the boys there certainly get to know the history of our game and that includes that very first game against Wales all those years ago. We also know of course that Deans did score that try! I am more acutely aware of it possibly because the captain that day, Dave Gallaher, was from the Ponsonby Club in Auckland, which is my club, so there's a special significance there for me too. From that game, we are conscious of the long heritage of the link that game established between Wales and New Zealand. Losing for an All Black is almost sacrilege and right from that first tour, that game entered into our folklore because it hurt us. Now, we're pleased it happened, because from it came a special relationship that has lasted since then and it forged a rugby camaraderie. I also think that rugby has played a very similar role in both countries in terms of giving two small nations a way of making a name for themselves. We can both compete at the highest world level because of rugby. Both nations understand that about the other, which contributes further to the relationship between us in a way it might not between us and some other countries.'

So, the special relationship was forged. A relationship that grows from every encounter between the teams to this day, that makes each visit of the touring Kiwis more eagerly anticipated than the previous one. Wales enjoyed a degree of success against the touring New Zealanders. Before playing Llanelli, the All Blacks had lost seven games on British soil, six of them either to Wales or Welsh clubs.

Fox, Bogle and Hoskins sum up the impact of 1905 in this way: 'The fact that Wales won what many consider to be the greatest international game of all time, plus the controversy surrounding the Deans incident, has forged a special bond between New Zealanders and the Welsh. While rivalry is fierce on the field of play, a mutual love of the game has ensured a lasting respect between two nations that view rugby football as the finest of sports.'

The road to 1972 started in 1905 – the first Wales victory against the All Blacks and the last victory against them on Welsh soil. When Bryan Williams and the seventh All Blacks left New Zealand shores, they knew exactly where they were going. 'We had a long four-and-a-half-month tour ahead of us,' says Bryan Williams, 'and we knew that we would face our toughest test in Wales. They were the greatest power of all, who had already beaten us three times on previous tours. We knew full well that it's in Wales that we would be up against it. We had also seen the Lions play in '71 and had seen for ourselves some of the individuals we would be up against and, of course, in Llanelli's case, they had the Lions coach at the helm. People have suggested that we were well up for revenge for the Lions defeat when we got to Britain in '72. I'm not so sure it was that. It was much more to do with the fact that we needed to get back to our own winning ways immediately. It's what the All Blacks do. But we knew the ultimate challenge would be in Wales.'

6

The working
man's game

In Wales what is special is small-country psychology – a special kind
of need for heroes that could reassure us of our existence as a country.

Rhodri Morgan, former Wales First Minister

EVERY ONE OF the 15 on the pitch that October day could sing
along quite heartily with Rita McNeil, 'It's a working man I
am...'. Not all of them would have carried tin lunch-boxes in
their hands or felt dust settle on their lungs, but they all had
a day job. Maybe that's one of the biggest surprises in looking
back at the 1972 game because in this age of professional,
regional, high-gloss rugby, we've forgotten what rugby was
really like in those days. And this is not to venture down that
contentious alleyway of deciding which era was the best. Let's
just remember what the Seventies era was like for the stars
that played and scaled the heights of the amateur game.

There was quite a variety of jobs amongst the fifteen on the
pitch and those on the bench. Many earned their crust in the
industrial tradition outlined in the first chapter. Unbeknown
to them, that tradition was seeing its last days. But in October
'72, it was still a working reality.

Gareth Jenkins feels an obvious pride in his link with
Llanelli's steel story. Fresh from school, he had an engineering
apprenticeship with the British Steel Corporation who

then owned the Machynys Works, one of those founded by Morewood and Rogers before the rugby club was formed. Today, the site is home to the Jack Nicklaus designed golf course at the Machynys Peninsula Golf and Country Club. A far cry from what life was like even 40 years ago.

'There were 350 men working in Machynys then, all tradesmen. It was the engineering centre for servicing all other BSC plants. We would make all the big fabrication hardware, such as ladles and ingot carriers, for Trostre, Port Talbot, Llanwern, Shotton and so many more steel plants. By the time the All Blacks came, I had finished my apprenticeship and had moved to what was then called Duport Steel, but everyone in the town still called the Klondike. That was a fantastic place to work, with over 3,000 men employed there. Thank goodness, looking back at that time now, I was able to experience a moment of actually being in the industrial heart of the town. That's honestly what it feels like, a very proud feeling of being part of something that was so central to the shaping and making of Llanelli.'

Gareth was by then part of the actual steel-making process. And his co-workers were also very much a part of Gareth's playing career. 'It was so difficult to go to work after a bad game! I worked Sundays a lot and could be back in work at eight in the morning on the day after a heavy loss on the Saturday. Actually, it didn't have to be a heavy loss; it could be your individual performance that was under the cosh! They'd call you all names and it got quite heated. That's how accountable we were.'

On the Monday before playing the All Blacks, Gareth was called to deal with a particular problem that had cropped up in the Klondike. 'I was given a bitch of a job that Monday morning. I was called on to repair a major problem with an ingot stopping gate. In order to deal with it, I had to go underneath the whole thing, in a very confined space and in sweltering heat. My clothes were as wet as if I had stood out in a thunderstorm for hours. If you had to do what was called 'wet work', it was job and finish. I started on it at six in the morning and finished at eleven and was allowed to go home. But it was a dangerous, grafting, physical work which took so long to do. There was certainly no regard for the fact that I was playing against the All Blacks the day after!'

The Klondike would have made special working arrangements for the Tuesday afternoon of the game. Being a processing plant, it couldn't shut down completely or the steel would be totally wasted. But it reduced to a skeleton staff and slowed the steel-making process down. Another of the Scarlet heroes worked in the Klondike at that time too. Although, things could have been so different if the ugly side of heavy industry hadn't affected Phil Bennett's family. 'I was offered a scholarship at Llandovery College when I was about 15, by Carwyn James. At the same time, some football clubs were interested in me as well. But my father had a nasty accident in the steel works, so all those offers meant nothing to me. At fifteen I went into the steel industry myself, so that I could help support the family. That was a massive culture shock. I went from being in school, playing for the school team and for Wales' schoolboys to the heavy working world of steel. But once I got used to it, it was without doubt the greatest university I could possibly have gone to. I mixed with all sorts of men, with all sorts of interests, backgrounds and intelligence.'

Phil Bennett was what was termed a clay boy in the steel works, part of a well-established hierarchy which included the labourers one step above him and the brickies, another step up again. His job was to make sure that there was enough clay available for the labourers to make bricks for the brickies. That was quite some production line as it was a huge building. Gareth Jenkins and Phil Bennett were in a long line of Scarlets players who worked at the Klondike. It was a tradition they were very much aware of as Phil Bennett notes. 'Many of the Llanelli greats worked there: Gruff Bevan, Howard Davies, Stan Williams, Ossie Williams and, of course, the legendary Welsh rugby star of the Twenties, Albert Jenkins. They represented so many thousands of Llanelli men who knew nothing else but the steel works and Stradey. The men worked hard during the week and what kept them going was the chance to have a few pints with their mates, and going to Stradey on a Saturday afternoon. That's what they lived for.'

From this tradition came the name 'men of steel' when referring to Llanelli Rugby Club. One other player in October '72 worked in the same industry, but at a different plant. Roy 'Shanto' Thomas worked for British Steel at their Velindre works, near Swansea, although he had worked in a completely different place before that. 'I come from Penclawdd, the small Gower village known for its cockles, in particular. I worked for a while in that seafood industry if you like, in a small shop in Penclawdd selling cockles, laver bread and fish for about a year probably. People used to come from far to buy a brace, which was actually three flat fish, one not so big and two big ones. I had a coal business once as well and a few other jobs, before going to Velindre.'

In the steel works, Shanto had the wonderful title of head baller. It actually meant being part of a team collecting all the scrap steel which was cut off from the coil of steel and crushing it into a ball. But to anyone who knows the colourful character Shanto, that title certainly has comic irony to it! He treasures two things from his coal miner stepfather: his nickname and a rather unusual gold medal. 'My dad worked in the mines and was responsible for the shunting of coal drams back and forth underground. He got the name the Great Shanto because of that and I got the name after him. He has quite a claim to fame as well. He won the first gold medal at the Empire Games in Cardiff in 1958. I keep people guessing for hours in pubs as to what he won it for, and nobody has ever guessed it. He got it for winning the first race which marked the official opening of the games – a pigeon race! My dad's bird won it and he got the gold! I've still got the medal to this day. So he had his sporting achievement as well.'

When it came to arranging time off to play against the

All Blacks, Shanto had to go to another rugby legend, Brian Thomas, the manager at Velindre Works. He captained and coached Neath and played his last game for Wales out in Auckland against New Zealand in 1969. Under his management Neath won the Welsh club Championship five times. He passed away in 2012. There was always the usual friendly banter from Brian when Shanto would go to negotiate time off, but it was never refused and Shanto praises the support he got from one who was such a rugby playing legend himself.

Shanto's nickname was just one link that the '72 team members had with the coal industry, however, not one of the members of the team was directly involved with working in coal mines. Many, though, would have had strong family ties with that industry.

One who would have been tightly bound to Shanto in the scrums was the prop on his shoulder, Tony Crocker. He worked for the so-called new heavy industry in Llanelli, the car industry, for Morris Motors. The famous Morris motoring brand began in Oxford in 1912, creating all the famous Morris cars that were such a part of the car revolution in Britain. They moved to many places from Oxford, including opening a factory in Llanelli. In 1968 Morris Motors were taken over by British Leyland Motor Corporation, a name that would become synonymous with much of the industrial unrest that blighted the 1970s.

By the time the All Blacks were in town, Tony Crocker had worked at the Llanelli plant which made car radiators and seats for a couple of years, starting work there when he was 21. He worked days and for the maintenance teams in the factory. 'There had been so much hype and excitement all week; I think the bosses were glad to see me go to the match itself on the Tuesday. None of us knew what the result would be then of course, so little did they know that the excitement would get worse on Wednesday!'

As has been established, rugby had become the working man's game in Wales early on, more so in Wales than in any other of the home nations. Indeed, when Wales started to succeed on the international field, winning that first Triple Crown in 1893, the other countries accused Wales of unfairly taking advantage of the supply of burly miners and steel workers available to them for selection. It was claimed that was an unfair advantage!

Rugby also caught hold of the working man in Wales in the face of the rise in popularity of football as well. Wales' Premier League club, Swansea, are celebrating their centenary this year. But that was 40 years after the formation of those first rugby clubs, despite the fact that the FA was already up and running when the WRU was formed in Wales. Dai Smith sums it up in this way, 'What was odd in the Welsh experience was not the absorption of Association Football from industrial Lancashire and Yorkshire in north Wales but the manner in which an amateur public-school game took root, in such a lasting fashion, in the south. Indeed rugby in its early days was not well-liked by those who saw it as another aspect of the intrusion of a non-Welsh secular world.'

But, even with the working man so prominent, the old taunt about forwards being piano shifters and the backs being piano players would have some resonance with the pioneer players. There were those who played and who didn't get their hands dirty during the week – no doubt some forwards would say so during the game as well! In Llanelli's '72 team, there were three teachers and two students on the field of play, and a couple of teachers on the bench as well.

'I started teaching in 1970 at a junior school in Newport,' explains prop forward Barry Llewellyn, whose brother Bryan was on the subs bench for the All Blacks game, 'but by October '72 I was a PE teacher at Green Hill Comprehensive in Tenby. I had also, in the previous July, opened a sports shop in the town, with Carwyn James and Barry John officially opening it. I carried on teaching and running the shop for a while until it got to the point that I was almost paying someone more to run the shop than I was earning teaching! So the shop took over.'

J.J. Williams and Roy Bergiers were also PE teachers: J.J. in Maesteg and Roy in Carmarthen. Full back Roger Davies was a student at Trinity College, Carmarthen and Hefin Jenkins was at the Glamorgan College of Technology, now the University of Glamorgan in Trefforest. Previously, it had been the School of Mines, teaching the fundamentals of mining in the heart of the south Wales coalfield. The main house, which was the School of Mines, had previously been the home of the Crawshay family, who built foundries and gave their name to a representative rugby team.

Hefin recalls, 'I was in my final year studying estate management and living in some hovel-like students' housing in Cardiff with a gang of other students. On the night before the game, I stayed at my parents' house, where I was brought up, in Burry Port. On the way over to meet the team that morning, I stopped at a kiosk on the council estate to make a phone call. There was no phone in my parents' house in those days. One of the main men in Llanelli at the time was the clerk of the council and he suggested I ring a certain number to ask about the possibility of work when I finished college. I thought I'd better do it there and then as I'd probably not have much time later on!'

Roger Davies was in his first year at Trinity College, Carmarthen, but he'd gone to college later, having worked for some years first. He worked for 3M's engineering company in Gorseinon and then the Morganite Company in Swansea. Morganite made carbon brushes for the motor industry. After leaving he went to do a teacher training course in Carmarthen. 'I nearly missed the game against the Barbarians because it was on the same day as enrolment at college. I went to enrol and there was such a queue it took a really long time for my turn to come. Angela, my girlfriend at the time, now my wife, had come down from Aberystwyth to see the game and was sitting in the stand not sure if I had arrived or not. She insists to this day that I ran on the pitch tying my shorts up and tucking my shirt into them!'

Both J.J. Williams and Roy Bergiers were caught up in the sometimes difficult situation of having to arrange time off to play in games. J.J. remembers, 'The week of the All Blacks game was half-term with us, but not in Carmarthenshire. I was asked to take an athletics course at Ogmore School camp, which was a camp used for all sorts of sports courses. I was there all day on the Monday before the game. I went home Monday night and travelled to Llanelli on the Tuesday morning, having had the day off officially. But I ended up taking the Wednesday off as well, because we'd won and went back on the course on Thursday and Friday. But they refused to pay me for the week because I had taken leave without permission on the Wednesday. I was refused pay for the entire length of the Lions tour in 1974, three months of it! That's when I left teaching and started my own business and I haven't looked back since.'

Roy Bergiers also had to go without money to play in that game, but with a slightly different twist. 'I suppose I was a new, young, conscientious teacher and had asked for the Tuesday off through the official channels way in advance of the day. I was given the time, but without pay. By the time of the game, the education authority had not given a blanket day off to every school in the county, but had given a directive that headmasters could use their discretion as to whether to allow staff and pupils to go or not. Many of my fellow teachers went to the game, as did many school children. But the irony of the whole thing is that they had a few hours off in the afternoon with full pay to watch me play in a team who beat the All Blacks, and I wasn't paid at all!'

There were indeed many disgruntled teachers in schools throughout the county who couldn't go because the headmaster refused to grant permission, and their school day continued as normal. They were even more displeased when they found out the score.

The captain and the youngest player did the same work, one in Carmarthen and the other in Llanelli. Delme Thomas and Grav were both electricity linesmen, climbing up the electricity poles day in, day out. 'I worked from 8 till 4,' recalls Delme Thomas, 'the same pattern of work every day, climbing those poles whatever the weather. But I suppose it did make us a little bit tougher.'

At that time many rugby players were turning to work as reps for various companies. It offered a flexibility that seemed to suit the demands of work and rugby. Derek Quinnell was one of these. 'The match programme put me down as an electrician, but in fact I worked then as a rep for a British fertilizer company. This meant travelling up to Scotland, the Midlands, and the north-east, everywhere. I travelled a heck of a lot with that job, but I loved it. The usual pattern was to come back from wherever I was straight to Stradey for training, and then back to see the wife and the family after that. I did that for three years, but even though I enjoyed it, it proved impossible to balance it with rugby and family. On the day before the All Blacks game I would have made sure that I was fairly local and we would have trained at Stradey on the Sunday too.'

Chico Hopkins was a PR officer for Everwarm Homes throughout Wales. This meant he travelled extensively to meet representatives of local authorities, trying to persuade them to use Everwarm central heating. 'Councils then had a Rent Option Scheme, where they would install central heating systems in their council houses and offer to pay something like 50p a week of the heating bills. My job was to persuade them to use our heating systems when they installed central heating in their houses. It was a good time to do that work because things were changing fast in the energy world and council houses were changing over to central heating systems in a big way for the first time. I had great support from my employers. My boss even used to lend me his Mercedes to go to matches. The club officials always used to give us travelling expenses, but they'd always work out exactly how far we'd travelled and give us what we were due, and no more. What they didn't take into account was the fact that quite often I was using the boss' car, which he put the petrol into, and I pocketed the expenses!'

Andy Hill was also involved with a local authority and council houses, but as a rent collector for Swansea council. He'd worked for a short period in the Klondike Steel Works in Llanelli, but that was, in his own words, 'too much of a culture shock' and by the time of the game, he was working with Swansea council. 'I collected rent from houses in the Penlan, Portmead, Blaen y Maes and Townhill areas, some of the areas that people today give a bad name to, and often rightly so. But, I must say that I loved the people I would meet in those places. There was not a lot of money in those houses at all, but the people were so honest and warm. I lived in Penlan myself, with my parents then, and I loved the open spaces that were around the estates.'

As we've heard already, Tom David worked for British Airways, or at least a subsidiary company owned by them called British Engine Overhaul Ltd. Tom was a technician with them, working in Trefforest, near Pontypridd. He too enjoyed full support from his employers when it came to time off, with pay for matches. But he also had other backing at his workplace as well. 'In the factory at Trefforest, we had two medical sisters in a medical unit there. If I had any injury, I could go down for treatment during the week while I was in work. That, and their backing with time off, was the way that BEO Ltd. showed their own particular commitment to rugby in Wales.'

Back in the world of steel and the traditional heavy industries, Phil Bennett also remembers clearly how the players received all sorts of support, other than from the terraces on a Saturday afternoon. 'When I had the injury which meant I didn't go to see the All Blacks playing Western Counties, I went for treatment with the club's much loved physio, Bert Peel. But that was not at Stradey. I used to go up to Cwmgwili Colliery near Cross Hands, where Bert worked. I felt so proud going there, especially if a visit coincided with the miners coming off shift and seeing them come to the surface with blackened faces and go straight to the pithead baths. Bert would treat me right next to the baths, and I could feel the heat and the

The town gets ready with floral and shop displays.

The band of the 1st Battalion Royal Welsh Fusiliers build up the atmosphere.
Photo: © Alan T. Richards

The Alan Richards original team photo, with Grav looking at him, not any one else.
Photo: © Alan T. Richards

Under-12s – oblivious to film crews, the crowd and even the All Blacks. They've got a game to play!
Photo: © Alan T. Richards

Game on, and it's early Llanelli pressure.
Photo: © Alan T. Richards

The Llanelli strength, the line-out.
Photo: © Alan T. Richards

A rare All Black attack in the first half.
Photo: © Alan T. Richards

Another Llanelli win at the line-out.
Photo: © Alan T. Richards

J.J. and Hales in hands, knees and bumps-a-daisy.
Photo: © Alan T. Richards

What's Shanto doing there anyway?
Photo: © Alan T. Richards

Roger sends Andy away.
Photo: © Alan T. Richards

That one was close!
Photo: © Alan T. Richards

But this one was over and Andy does a one-off celebration straight into Tom's arms!
Photo: © Alan T. Richards

That's it! A famous victory secured.
Photo: © Alan T. Richards

The fans flood the pitch.
Photo: © Alan T. Richards

A captain is carried
triumphantly!
Photo: © Alan T. Richards

History is recorded.
Photo: © Alan T. Richards

Back in the dressing room, the captain is congratulated, again.
Photo: © Alan T. Richards

The only photo of Roy's try, in front of so many people he knew.
Photo: Roy Bergiers personal collection

LLANELLI TRIUMPH NO FLUKE

ALL BLACKS HUMBLED BY SUPER 'SCARLETS'

WALES GOES WILD!

Llanelli 9pts, All Blacks 3

LLANELLI skipper Delme Thomas was close to tears in the emotional aftermath of a dramatic victory by a side who produced the most inspired Rugby of their lives.

"I've played twelve years for Llanelli, but there's never been a day like this one," he told me.

Stradey Park was still packed with 22,000 delirious fans, still singing and cheering as they had throughout an often brutal battle.

By CHRIS LANDER

Counties on Saturday, were thoroughly out-   we've got the most loyal supporters.

All Blacks under pressure! Roy Thomas charges down a kick from New Zealander Lindsay Collins as the Welsh boys head for their glory win.

"We squeezed them . . never let them go"

of so much that went wrong for the New Zealanders.

Welsh and British papers salute Llanelli's win, and the captain reads of his team's triumph.

WESTERN MAIL

Wednesday, November 1, 1972   THE NATIONAL NEWSPAPER OF WALES

LLANELLI V. ALL BLACKS SPECIAL

No. 32,137   4p

BELLS SCOTCH WHISKY

Llanelli toasts its 15 heroes

By STEPHEN OLDFIELD

Town goes wild as All-Blacks fall

GROWN MEN hugged each other, danced in the streets, and wept unashamed tears of joy last night as Llanelli went wild after their historic 9-3 win over the All Blacks.

The town took on a Christmas carnival atmosphere as fans set out to drink the pubs dry, one jeweller said, "If there was some absenteeism today, wait for tomorrow. For us Christmas has come early."

The celebrations started with the mad within which thousands of ecstatic fans poured on to Stradey Park. Llanelli had reached the rugby hall of fame—the fourth Welsh club team in history to beat the mighty All Blacks.

The Llanelli captain Delme Thomas told his jubilant supporters as he was carried shoulder-high from the field: "This is the greatest day of my life."

It was a spectacular triumph for the side of Llanelli coach Carwyn James, who told me: "The celebrations were all smiles today."

They was praise too from New Zealand manager Ernie Todd, who said the Scarlets deserved to win a very hard game of rugby. The

no complaints and we will be back challenging again," he added.

The celebrations that followed were all too much for some publichouses, where taps had spilled out on to the pavements and tapemen each were ordering to song by off ecstasy.

And the whole scene was crowned with an act by Clyde Evans who placed his grip on the pavement under the bewildered gaze of a policeman to declare it fine of the greatest days in the history of Welsh rugby.

Mr. Evans, who travelled from Narberth for the game and seldom misses a Llanelli fixture in Wales, said, "We must now be acknowledged as the greatest club team in the world.

"The All Blacks were a good side. They won't be beaten a lot on this hour and then people will really understand what a magnificent win this was."

Many Llanelli followers were weightier as we had happier last night. One man was £12 after being given odds of 12-1 against his team's win and several others to whom I spoke had won large amounts. It was the most popular turn-up since the David and

One man who lost all on the result said that he had never been happier to see his money go.

Last word to Llanelli's hero of the hour Phil Bennett, who all saved real indignantly assumed the mantle of the great King John with yesterday's display.

He admitted that he had blinked back tears in the dressing room before going out to face his seventh All Black.

"I have heard many team talks from top coaches before a match but none one like this from our skipper Delme Thomas," said Bennett.

"He told us he had been all around the world and gained all the rugby honours possible. But he would willingly give them all away if only we could win the match for him."

Report and pictures—
Pages 16 and 18.

RIGHT : Llanelli captain Delme Thomas is lifted high among the sea of ecstatic fans after the Stradey triumph.

Roy Bergiers' shirt.
Photo: © Emyr Young

Bruce Robertson's shirt.
Photo: © Emyr Young

The match ball, signed by
both teams.
Photo: © Emyr Young

A victory that inspired
poetry and art.

Delme, Grogged, a rare piece.　　　　　　A rugby victory cast in brass.

Llanelli 9 - Seland Newydd 3

October 31st 1972

"And how is little Roy Carwyn Derek Delme Phil John today then?"

Les Williams at the centenary banquet on the pitch at Stradey.

Coach Carwyn James, captain Delme Thomas and chairman Handel Greville.

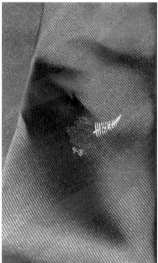

A collectors' item – commemorative tie.

Gareth Edwards, Barry John and Carwyn James at a centenary function.

Phil Bennett in front of a unique plaque to remember '72 at the Stradey Arms.

Max Boyce and J.J. relive the day, decades later!

Photo: J.J. Williams personal collection

Tommy David signs the team photo – 40 years on.

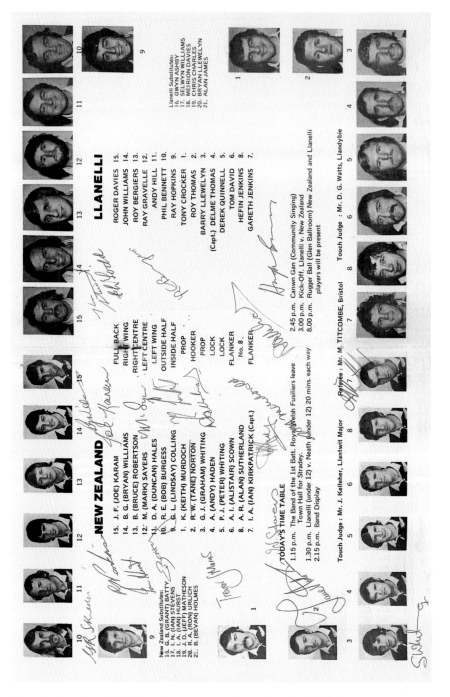

Llanelli schoolboy Mark Sayers' programme signed by the All Blacks.

steam coming from there. There was a man there helping him too, Cyril, who was a physio for the Ammanford club. And what I loved after that was to go for a breakfast in the colliery canteen with the miners. That was special. There was nothing underhanded about all this; it wasn't sneaking me in through the back door or anything. But the manager there was a Scarlets fan and it was his way of showing support.'

Rugby in that era was totally dependant on this kind of support. It would show itself in other ways in Llanelli too, with the steel works playing a central role. Phil continues, 'When I first played for Wales, I remember going to Ireland and the trip took four days in all. I was docked the full four days' pay at that time. Then a man started in the steel works called Eric McVicer, who only recently passed away this year. He changed the whole system in the works with regards to us rugby players. I was about to go off on a tour, it was probably with Llanelli to South Africa, and Eric wanted a word with me, saying he didn't think it right that I should go without pay. He knew I was fairly newly married with new responsibilities. He then went to meet the board of the works and argued that the rugby players were an asset to the company and should be recognised as such. There was no way that me getting paid to play rugby would result in any more steel being sold internationally, but there were ways the company and the industry could benefit by backing club players and Welsh internationals. Eric succeeded and turned things round completely.'

Eric McVicer also started a Llanelli Steel rugby team. They very rarely lost as there were always half a dozen or so Scarlets in the side. Eric also had the vision as to who the team should play against. He didn't see any use in them playing the local teams in the area who they all knew anyway. Phil adds, 'He arranged games with universities in Lampeter and Aberystwyth, for example. It was good experience for the students and for us it was invaluable too, as we would mix with totally different people that we were used to mixing with, either with Llanelli or our village teams. These boys were at Welsh universities, but they might well have come from any corner of Britain. We played Swansea Police too, and that meant the great Brian Butler up against Byron Gale, a Scarlet who was a policeman in Swansea – what a clash! Bernard Thomas played for us, John Coch, Alan Richards, Andy Hill, it was great! Eric believed in the importance of broadening our horizons. A man in the Klondike who was a 27-year-old labourer, for example, having been there since he was 15 could, on the rugby pitch, be up against a student who, in the following year, might be in London studying to be a barrister. Eric thought that was beneficial to us in the steel works, giving us a broader outlook in life. If Eric hadn't turned things round, I don't know what I personally would have been able to do in rugby. I wouldn't have been able to go on the Lions tour in 1974, for certain. No way could I have gone that long with no pay. When I was out there, Eric used to go up to the house to give Pat, my wife, my pay personally.'

The Llanelli Steel Works team played in People's Park, where that very first kick-about was instigated by the man running the tinplate works in the town. The '72 side echoed those early local teams like the Seaside Stars and the New Dock Stars, who were made up of men who worked the foundries. History was turning full circle. Tom Hudson, Norman Gale and Carwyn James were obviously influential individuals within the rugby set-up at Stradey. But another unexpected key individual, in his own unique way, was certainly Eric McVicer.

The Klondike and Stradey were very close to each other geographically. As far as the workers were concerned they were almost inseparable. The week's sweat and toil was endured with two things in mind: a few pints with their mates, and that Saturday afternoon pilgrimage to see Llanelli play at Stradey. That was the pattern. Many, of course, would go straight from the steel works to Stradey if they worked Saturday morning, and that would include the players. The support was also extremely practical according to Phil Bennett. 'The amount of maintenance work that the men did at Stradey free of charge is phenomenal. They literally saved the club thousands of pounds in those days. The brickies would rebuild any wall free of charge, the containing bars needed for the spectator areas would be made in the works, and any repairs to the stand were done by the steel men. And they would do this very often during work time, as foremen and managers would give them time off to do it. Or they would do it in their own time, of course. I remember turning up for training one night and one of the boys from work was building a brick wall which was quite big. He would be there night after night, doing it in return for a flagon of cider! I have no doubt, strange as it may seem to people now who don't remember that kind of world, that a huge part of my pride after beating the All Blacks, came from the link that victory had with a tradition like this.'

7

The players' game

What always attracted me [to rugby] was the thrill; some would
say the brown-trousered terror... Humiliation or glory, pain
or ecstasy, lie ahead. But which will it be?

Spike Milligan, comedy legend who lists
Phil Bennett in his top 6 best rugby players of all time

i Players get ready

In 1972 there was many a big battle. It was David Bowie's
Ziggy Stardust versus the world; David Cassidy versus Donny
Osmond; the Harlem Globetrotters versus everyone else; black
versus white on the *Love Thy Neighbour* TV series; Glam Rock
versus parents; Action Man versus G.I. Joe, without forgetting
of course, the other matter of Prime Minister Ted Heath versus
the miners, and it was definitely that way round in south
Wales.

Action Man was the toy of the year in 1972, but for thousands
and thousands of hardened rugby fans, there was no question
that the real action men that year wore scarlet. Waking on that
Tuesday morning, twenty-one players on each side would no
doubt have had conflicting and varying thoughts and emotions
going through their minds. For Llanelli star, Phil Bennett, the
day started with his usual daily routine. 'That morning, I got
up after having slept quite well, really. And, as usual, I left the
house about eight o'clock to walk over to the paper shop, about
20 yards across the road from where we lived. As I walked that
fairly short distance, whoever I happened to pass would look at

me and say, "All right Phil?" "How are you today Phil?" Normal enough comments, but they gave me a strange feeling that day. It was as if there was an extra significance behind what they were asking; it was more pointed, with weight on every word. I thought to myself, there's something strange here! There was an air of nervousness. In the shop I asked for my paper and the guy in the shop was the same as everyone else, "How you feeling Phil?" I got back to the house and told Pat that that short journey had really got to me. I wasn't feeling nervous before that. That normally would have kicked-in a lot later. It was really nice to have a couple of hours in the house then to escape all this, to shut myself off from it all. That helped a lot, and then Pat drove me to meet the rest of the boys.'

The players who lived outside Llanelli were spared this nervous intensity. Chico, Tom David and J.J. came from further east that morning. Roger Davies picked up Andy Hill as they both came in from Swansea, Roy Thomas came from Penclawdd, and Delme and Roy came for Carmarthen. They all remember that it was seeing the crowds beginning to walk towards the ground from the outskirts, mid-morning, which made that early impression on them as to how big an occasion they were about to play a part of. Sleep had been very much on student Roger Davies' mind in preparation for the game. 'I knew that I would get very little sleep if I stayed in the halls of residence in the days before playing, so I went to my parents' house in Swansea to make sure I'd get a good night's sleep. When I got to Stradey I met two guys in the car park who I knew from Mumbles. They were down looking for tickets but unfortunately I couldn't help them.'

'We probably came together as a squad a lot more often in the run-up to that game than we normally would otherwise,' says Derek Quinnell, 'and that continued at the very start of the day itself. Carwyn wanted us all together early that morning. So we gathered at Stradey and a coach took us to the Ashburnham Hotel in Burry Port where it was to be a mix of time to focus together, to listen to others talking to us and a bite to eat as well. On match days, I usually had something small for breakfast, like beans on toast and very little else. But there was food at the Ash as well.'

The student in him influenced Roger Davies again at the Ash. 'There was a free meal on offer after all! I had the chance of having steak, something which wasn't very common in those days, yet alone for a student, so I would have been foolish to turn it down!'

'I had no idea what it meant to eat or not to eat a meal before a game at all,' adds Gareth Jenkins, 'after all, a meal was a meal! And when Tilly, the Scottish manager of the hotel (which was the posh, special place to go those days), said he'd ordered the finest Angus steak, it just had to be eaten. In today's terms, it was the worse thing we could ever, ever have done!'

There's one more culinary moment that has stayed clearly in Gareth Jenkins' mind from that time at the hotel as well. 'I'll never forget that Delme asked for a sherry! Grav and I were sitting together, the two youngest in the team, we were pals. Next thing, Delme asked for an egg and broke the raw egg into the sherry and downed it in one. Grav and I looked at each other in sheer amazement, never having seen anything like that before. We concluded that Delme must have done that when he played for Wales and the Lions as well, and that's what heroes did to prepare for big matches. He was so much our hero, Grav and me, that all Delme did was accentuated.'

Roy Bergiers, having had a lift in Delme's Wolsley from Carmarthen, was similarly awestruck and found the journey to the game to be a surreal experience. 'Here was this Welsh international forward giant, three times a British Lion, winner of a Test series out in New Zealand, and he was my chauffeur! How bizarre was that for me sitting next to him. Then, as we came to the bottom of Llandyfaelog hill, just before Kidwelly, I saw a magpie chasing a big crow. I remember casually thinking to myself, well, there's bad luck for the All Blacks today then! Strange how the day turned out after that.'

Contrary to many other players, however, Roy had studied

the dietary aspect of physical exercise in college and knew what not to eat before a game. 'I had learned that it was best not to eat because the blood would basically take to dealing with the food and away from muscle performance. But what could I do with a steak in front of me? I nibbled at it, bit by bit, thinking I'd have a small corner, but the whole lot went in the end – so much for the science!'

Other players seem to forget what they had to eat that morning, with many saying they had nothing. A central part of that morning was the speeches given by various individuals. Again, the mists of time have clouded exact memories for the players. Many mention people who gave a speech, who've then since said themselves that they actually weren't there – Clive Rowlands, for example. After some talking, the players were getting more and more wound up. The shrewd Carwyn James noticed this and dealt with the situation immediately. 'Carwyn noticed, I think, that we were heading to go through the roof a little too soon,' Phil Bennett recalls, 'especially after Norman shared a few of his not-so-choice, direct, words with us. So he took us all out for a walk, to ease the tension a little bit.'

'He took us over to the Ashburnham Golf Club, across the road a little from the hotel,' Roger Davies adds, 'and we went for a short walk there to get some fresh air. We'd been at the golf club together the night before as well.'

What follows next has proven to be the one main talking point when discussing the game with the players for this book. Delme Thomas has entered rugby folklore, not only for captaining the winning side, but for the speech that he gave before the game. But where did he give that speech? The players remember differently. Some say at the Ashburnham, some say in the dressing room at Stradey. The consensus is clearly in favour of the Ashburnham, which is what Delme recalls himself. What is in no doubt whatsoever is the content of the speech and its impact 40 years later. Delme recalls the Ashburnham morning in full. 'I had been telling the boys off and on for years about playing against New Zealand. I had toured with the Lions there in 1966 and 1971 and I always used to say back at Stradey, "Listen boys, until you've played the All Blacks you haven't played rugby!" It became a bit of a running joke in the end, but in '72 it was the time when they would actually face the All Blacks on the pitch. Most of them hadn't any idea what I meant, of course. Playing against the All Blacks is what every child dreamt about. I had played against legends like Waka Nathan, Don Clarke and Winston Whineray. I played against them in 1966 as an uncapped Lion, as Derek did in 1971. That's the Test series I treasure because, even though we lost, it was my first and we played against legends.

'In the Ash, we had lunch about elevenish I think. Some others had an invite too, club chairman Handel Greville was there and Ray Williams, from the WRU. They shared a few words, then Carwyn spoke. I was then asked to tell the boys what I expected from them. Now was the time for me to bring them back to what I had been saying for years, that they hadn't played rugby until they'd played the All Blacks. This was the day that was going to happen. I told them that they would experience something that day that they had never experienced in their lives before.

'Most teams who play against the All Blacks are beaten before they get on the pitch. That was one thing I kept telling the boys in my talk at the Ashburnham. You've got to think you can win. Put it in your minds; get your heads in the right place that you're going to win. I know it will be tough. Half of you will be carried off, because it will be that bloody hard. But don't worry about that if you can read in the *Western Mail* the following day that you've beaten the All Blacks. And if anything does happen to you on the field, don't worry, there will be plenty there to carry you off! That's what we have to do. It's not too late to think like that now, but at half past four this afternoon it will be too late. It's there for the taking. It's a chance of a lifetime and most of you won't get a chance to play against the All Blacks again, so make it count.

'I said I had been lucky to be capped for Wales and been

on three Lions tours. But none of that meant anything to me. This was the day I wanted more than anything else. It wasn't in a foreign country; it was in front of our own crowd. We knew Stradey would be packed with supporters who showed passion like no one else. I said that you could keep all the Welsh caps and the Lions jerseys. This is what I wanted – to beat the All Blacks at Stradey. That would mean more to me than anything else I had achieved in the game. The boys listened very well, and some of the younger ones, like Grav and Budgie, were looking aghast at me, dumbfounded. But I could tell they were with me, they were where I wanted them to be. Carwyn said very little after that, just that I had said pretty much everything, so, he said, "Let's do it!"'

The following morning a headline on the back page of the *Western Mail* summed up the effect of that speech – 'Brilliant Delme Talk had me in Tears, says Phil'. Today, Phil says simply, 'I was crying, crying like a baby'.

'As Delme was speaking,' Roy Bergiers adds, with goose bumps on his arms, recalling the story forty years later, 'he made you think of people you knew in the villages around and the army of volunteers who were responsible for keeping the club going. He pulled on history and hiraeth in equal measure and then made it very personal. It was amazing, emotionally very powerful.'

The team left the Ashburnham, focused and fired up. Carwyn had instilled in them over a long period of time a strong sense of belief in themselves. After seeing the All Blacks at Gloucester he was even more convinced that they were beatable and he had the players to do it. The press reports of the Western Counties game had been published by then. They made foreboding reading: 'Black is Beautiful' said Clem Thomas, simply, in the *Observer*. 'Super size, strength, power and speed allied to rugby know-how' was how Wilf Wooller summed it up in the *Sunday Telegraph*. And Viv Jenkins in the *Sunday Times* had a message, 'Rugby men of Britain, you have been warned. Forget all that complacency after the victories of the 1971 Lions in New Zealand and any euphoria that came about as a result.'

But the mastermind of that 1971 success in New Zealand was now on a bus from Burry Port to Llanelli, and he didn't know what complacency meant. They were on their way to the ground to play against New Zealand, led by police outriders, and Carwyn knew that he had the men to beat them – again.

Looking out of those bus windows, no one had seen anything like it in a club match situation before. All the players say that seeing the people walking in their hordes from every direction, in the one direction of Stradey, made a huge impact on them. Phil Bennett says that what went through his mind simply was, 'We can't let these people down.'

'It looked like there were millions of people everywhere,' Tom David recalls, 'I could tell, even as one who had been brought into the club from another one, what this meant to the people of this area. That was so obvious on that bus journey down and no doubt at all that Carwyn had that in his mind when he decided we arrived at Stradey together by coach.'

'Seeing the people in the streets in their thousands as we travelled was also new,' says Delme. 'When we got to Stradey, with thousands more there in the car park, the boys got off the bus, totally focused. No one was distracted by the crowds, taken in by the emotion of it. Off the bus and into the dressing room. That's what I wanted and that's what we did. This was again a case of keeping the mind right. We could have been 110 per cent physically fit, but if the mind wasn't right, no good, mentally stale was no good.'

While all this was going on for the Llanelli team, the All Blacks were quietly making their way from Swansea. They hadn't had much time to train, having got to their hotel the Sunday night, leaving Monday for their coaching session.

'To be honest, we were cock-a-hoop coming from the Western Counties game,' says Bryan Williams. 'We'd followed the tradition of having one or two beers on the Sunday after the match, before travelling west and arriving very relaxed at the

Dragon Hotel. Having already said that we knew Wales would be tough, we were unfortunately too relaxed for our own good in the preparation for that game against Llanelli. When we got off the bus, we couldn't believe the people there in the car park, the crowds everywhere. We knew that this would be different, then.'

Once in the dressing room, the players on both sides went about their usual pre-match routine as they did for every game. For the Scarlets, that was only broken once. 'Word got out that the All Blacks' bus had arrived,' recalls Derek Quinnell, 'We could stand on the fixed benches that we sat on normally in the changing room, and look out through a narrow window high up in the wall. This looked out over the front car park. They walked off, looking stern and poker faced.'

'They had been to Canada before coming to Britain,' Gareth Jenkins adds, 'and some of them had bought hats out there. I think these were the inner circle of players who were called the Mafia by their own people in New Zealand. They looked menacing coming off the bus wearing what looked like cowboy hats. They had the stride, the strut and the swagger!'

As it turned out, those hats caused some unease within the All Black camp itself. Some of the management felt that wearing them detracted from the image that the All Blacks should portray on tour, that it almost showed that they didn't take it seriously. So, for the New Zealand authorities, wearing the hats lightened the tension too much, but for the Scarlets, it gave them a more menacing look. Bryan Williams explains the 'hat incident' from their perspective.

'There was a gang of us in the back seat who wore hats and I was one of them. Two of us, me and Sid Going, wore berets and the other three, Sutherland, Wylie and Norton, wore some kind of sombrero hat. Apparently, the sombrero look was interpreted as a bit menacing by many. The truth of the matter was that we were doing it in a light enough spirit and something was made out of nothing. Having said that, if the culture and the management of the tour party were as it should be, and we were all on the same wavelength, we would have chosen the appropriate time to wear those hats. Coming off planes and buses might not have been the right time. Good teams realise when to have fun and when not to. We didn't.'

'We weren't allowed to stand there for too long watching them, mind,' Roger Davies says. 'Carwyn soon put a stop to that, telling us not to be distracted by them and to get on with our own preparations. I was very nervous by then.'

'Carwyn took me out to the pitch about half hour before the game,' says Delme. 'I hadn't changed or anything, but Carwyn wanted me to feel the atmosphere in the crowd at that time. The band of the Welsh Guards was playing; the nanny goat was on the pitch. I'd never felt an atmosphere like it in my life. I had never seen Stradey like it. You could feel the emotion and the tension. The band could be heard from the dressing room, which added to the atmosphere. I looked around Stradey and knew that the people there were from the surrounding villages. I knew so many of them. That meant more to me than any international – knowing what it meant for them. How many thought we were going to beat the All Blacks I don't know, but they were there!'

The team then went out to the pitch to have a photograph taken. A bank of photographers from all over Britain was waiting for them. That was the first time the team saw the crowd and tasted the atmosphere. Their faces in the photograph show the fixed stares of an ashen-faced group of players. If you knew nothing of the team talks and the months of build-up which had made them confident they could win, that photo would give you exactly the opposite impression. It was to prove intimidating for some of the players, but Carwyn ushered them all back in as soon as was possible, so that the atmosphere didn't get to any of them in a destructive way. For some, it actually helped to calm the nerves before going out again for the match itself.

There was time for a few more speeches, with Delme topping up his Ashburnham talk with a shorter, more direct one. But this speech too had its effect. 'He certainly fired me up in the dressing room, as it did for a lot of us,' Barry Llewelyn recalls, 'We were ready to walk straight out, I think the forwards in particular got fired up in that dressing room chat.'

'Delme also pointed to a lot of us individually there, making points that related to us,' adds Phil Bennett. 'The last one he addressed was Grav, who had already done his usual routine of singing Welsh songs at the top of his voice, going to the toilet with his own toilet roll, and after a few minutes we could hear the flush and Grav banging the toilet door with his head! But when Delme turned to him and said in Welsh, "Ray, y crwt o Mynyddygarreg, ti 'da fi heddi, Ray!" you could see the pride swell up in his big frame. The two youngest players, Ray and Gareth, could have walked out, side by side, through any brick wall after that!'

ii Their finest hour

The game, in a nutshell, is quite easy to sum up. Llanelli went ahead in the first five minutes of the game. The All Blacks were finding life very difficult in the line-out and they lost the first four, giving a penalty away in the fourth. Phil Bennett's penalty kick, from over 40 yards, hit the post. The clearance kick by scrum half Lindsay Colling was charged down by Roy Bergiers for a try. Phil Bennett converted. The All Blacks could have gone in at half time with points level, but full back Joe Karam kicked one penalty, but missed another – so it was 6–3 at half time. In the second half, Andy Hill kicked a monster 50-yard penalty to make it 9–3 and the Llanelli team hung on for their famous victory.

Newspaper reports of the game vary in the actual number of penalties and line-outs awarded by referee Mike Titcombe. The penalty count ranges from 33 to 40, with Llanelli being awarded the most by far. Whichever figure is actually correct, that's a very high penalty count indeed! Llanelli also won the majority of line-outs.

Not surprisingly, maybe, the one aspect of that whole All Blacks visit which the players themselves were the least clear about was the actual detail of the game itself. The general reaction was that it all happened so fast. But they all have their snippets of memories, cameos from that most famous day, which have stayed with them for four decades.

Substitute Selwyn Williams remembers leaving the dressing room and hearing someone calling him from the stand. 'It was Carwyn, calling across to me in Welsh, "Dere fan hyn Sel!" He called me to go and sit by him in the stand, and that's where I saw the game. Carwyn didn't say much throughout the whole 80 minutes, just sat there, smoking, and taking it all in. There was no such thing as passing messages to the players during the game then anyway, not like now. His work was done, and he left it to the boys to get on with it. The only time he said something specific was when Chico took a hefty blow from one of their players. He told me to start getting ready to go on if Chico didn't get back up on his feet quick enough. But he did, and that was the end of that.'

This is how the fourteen men on the pitch that day remember the occasion, with their match day programme pen pics to their names:

Roger Davies – Full Back

24, 5' 9", 12 st. Britain's top try scoring full back with 16 tries to his credit this season – well fitted for the modern game, very popular; formerly with Swansea, quiet and unassuming, student

I remember the first kick-off; Benny kicked a short one just over the 10-yard line. I don't know if it was deliberate, it probably was, and it gave us an early chance to smash into them. We had that early opportunity to tell them clearly that we were up for it. There were a few early scuffles too. It was a perfect start and they knew they were in a game.

In the game at Gloucester, Alastair Scown had a rampaging game for the All Blacks and ruined their half backs' play. We had a plan to deal with him and Barry was pulled out of a line-out and stood in Phil Bennett's position. When the ball came back to him, he ran straight at Scown, knocking him over and the rest of the boys rucked all over him. It was also a way for us to protect Phil.

From my point of view, at the back, I was keen to get my hands on the ball early. After what seemed like an age, the first kick came my way. I caught it cleanly and they were penalised for a late tackle. They tried to rough me up a bit and one of them tried to take the ball away from me. But I was absolutely determined to get back on my feet with the ball in my hands, so that I could show that I had caught it and kept it.

I didn't see much of the ball going forward, with only a few chances to put either J.J. or Andy away on the wings. I remember one big tackle I had to make on Duncan Hales in one of the few moves they had attacking forward.

Throughout the game, first and foremost, was the feeling of not wanting to let your team mates down, especially in a game like that. We succeeded in putting a lot of pressure on them all the way through the game. But I didn't think we had won the game until the final whistle had been blown, it was too dangerous to think it before then!

J.J. Williams – Right Wing

24, 5' 9", 11 st. Wing three-quarter with sizzling pace, represented Wales in the Commonwealth Games. Capped as an outside half at secondary school level, played three times for Wales 'B', also played for Welsh XV against Canada; native of Maesteg, played for Bridgend; school master

This was my first big occasion ever. The plan was to spread the ball wide and run at them in this way. That's what the '71 Lions had done of course, under Carwyn. But it just didn't work out like that. To an extent, the occasion, the emotion, took over and I don't think it was the day to play rugby, basically.

It was all about not making mistakes and not giving them a chance. That became even truer when we had those first points on the board so early on. It became a forward-orientated game with a strong defence. Basically, that's how you win big games, as I found out when I was an international and a British Lion myself later on. Carwyn had instilled in us that it doesn't matter how good you are, if you're making mistakes, you're always playing catch-up.

We just didn't make any mistakes. Phil controlled everything as did Delme and every player did their bit. We attacked them at the back line a lot. The line-out battle was certainly the biggest single decisive factor, with Derek, Delme and Hefin dominant. They never got their game going and they didn't have a plan B.

Carwyn had instilled in us the belief that we could beat the All Blacks; there was hardly another coach in the land who could have done that. He also had Delme, Derek and Chico there to back him up, players who were with him in 1971.

Roy Bergiers – Centre

22, 6' 1", 13 st. 8 lbs. Emerged as the find of the season, capped for Wales, replacing John Dawes, Lions skipper when he retired from international football, devastating tackler, very fast and destined to become one of the top stars in Welsh rugby; physical education schoolmaster

I hardly had time to shut out the terrific noise that was swirling round the cauldron of Stradey when we had that first penalty after about the fourth line-out. The forwards had done extremely well to manipulate the penalty in the first place, squashing the line-out as they did. This meant that, as it was our throw-in, we had to have the last man in the line-out, but when we compressed the line, Scown was caught isolated at the back. Derek was very shrewd there.

When Benny lined up for the penalty, we just took our usual positions to stop their counterattack should the kick fail. I was there ready to stop any break up the middle, near the left-hand post. I stood there and watched the ball kicked by Benny, drift and drift, and drift off the woodwork into Colling's arms. He was just getting used to the pace of the game himself and took one step too many before putting in his clearing kick. My arms went up, I managed to charge it down and the ball fell kindly after the charge down for me to ground it for a try! It was almost in slow motion; I could see where the ball was and could go for it with what felt like plenty of time. That was all in the moment.

Then I began to realise what had happened! As I got up I could see some of the children I taught at school sitting on the upturned pop crates which had been laid out for them beyond the dead ball line. In the crowd I recognised the headmaster of a primary school and a few other people I knew. That was quite a feeling. But, we had to get on with the game.

The All Blacks' frustration from then on was obvious. They couldn't find the space to do their moves as they had planned. The forwards as a unit were immense, each with their role individually as well. The rucking was extreme to say the least and their frustration turned to physicality that crossed the line often, with man and ball, or man without the ball, being aggressively rucked at every opportunity. The game as far as I was concerned, was over very, very quickly.

Phil Bennett – Outside Half
24, 5' 7", 11 st. Welsh Senior & Youth international – toured Australia, New Zealand with Welsh team; truly a fine player in the traditional Welsh style, steelworker

Taking to that field that day, it was obvious that this was the one chance we would have to beat the All Blacks. As it happened, it wasn't a classic game. Our forwards were totally magnificent, and never gave an inch. I could go for most of a game and not see much of them because they were scrummaging, but Tony Crocker, Shanto, Barry Llywelyn were running round the field like lunatics, 'Gimme the ball!' 'Gimme the ball!'

So, seeing that, and we were ahead thanks to Budgie's try, it was obvious to me that there was no point in spreading the ball about. Let's keep putting the ball behind them, kicking it long, and through that giving them the message, 'Right, if you're going to score a try you'll have to do it from 60 or 70 yards away.' And I could do that knowing that we had the defence to cope with it if it happened. So long passes were out – anything that could risk dropping the ball and then leaving them with a hack through to the line, had to be cut out.

As long as we were in the lead we were in control. So I saw my job then was to put up a few high balls, to trouble their full back, Joe Karam, and to always put the ball behind their star man, Bryan Williams. If he's turning round, so is everyone else. Close the space down. We didn't feel that the crowd were getting to us at all for playing that way – they might have expected our open game. They were with us and we felt it.

I will always remember – it will live with me for the rest of my life – the last main action, with only minutes to go. They broke on their right-hand side and somebody chipped the ball ahead. I caught the ball right in the corner. In a split second I was thinking, what shall I do? Running over the line into touch was the easiest thing to do because I was nearly on it anyway. Instinctively, I stopped where I was and turned, with an All Black bearing down on me. He flew at me; I moved to the side and just saw him fly past me and land on his face behind. I knew I had to go for gold and kick the ball to safety. It will live with me that kick, because I think it was probably the best kick of my whole life! I positioned the lace of the ball where I knew it needed to be for the best spin from a kick, and hit it with all my strength. Joe Karam was standing four or five yards in field and, as the ball travelled up field, spinning in and in as it went, he moved further and further in towards the touchline and the ball was safe.

After that I realised that the one who flew at me in the corner was Grant Batty, who was on instead of Bryan Williams. I remember thinking, 'Grant you daft bugger, coming at me like a kamikaze pilot like that!' Later on in life, he did call me all names, in fun of course, and say, 'You really had me that day!'

Chico Hopkins – Scrum Half

(There was no pen pic of Chico Hopkins in the match day programme. Over the years the story has been that he arrived at the club too late for it to be included. But he arrived after J.J. Williams and Tom David, who are included. It was an oversight. His pen pic was included in the programme for the next game at Stradey.)

I can remember lots of little things about the game to be honest. I can remember taking the ball in the first ten minutes right on the corner flag and passing a long pass out to Phil who kicked it to touch. Then, later on, going round the blind side, I put a grubber kick through and my bloody ankle got tapped, or I'm sure I would have scored in the corner!

Towards the end of the game, the ball needed to be away from our side of the pitch and in to theirs. The boys were shouting at me to get it up the field but, instead of passing it out to Phil, I went to kick it myself. I got caught as I did it, and the ball ended up in Ian Kirkpatrick's hands. He threw out a long pass to Grant Batty – it was forward but the ref didn't pick that up – and Batty kicked ahead into our corner. I thought oh no, I've messed this up here, he's going to score. But Phil was in the corner and caught the ball, and you've heard the rest already! Many a time, thinking of that, I've thought to myself, I'm not gay or anything, but I would have slept with Phil Bennett that night! I would have been hung otherwise if he hadn't saved the day! Brilliant football from Phil.

Andy Hill – Left Wing

27, 5' 10", 12st 3lbs, the club's record points' scorer – 315 points to date this season, Wales trials, Barbarian, and county player; a sprinter with a very good defence, noted for his round-the-corner kicking, draughtsman

I remember having the ball once or twice! In those days the wing used to put a lot of cross kicks in and I remember doing one or two of those. I certainly remember the tackling as it was a very physical game and unusually so; it was like that playing on the wing as well. In the second half, we had a penalty and Phil passed the ball for me to take it. When we were in South Africa as a club, I had an Achilles injury on their hard grounds, and it was only two weeks or so before the All Blacks game that I felt it was back to normal. Phil had done more kicking during the season because of that. But I knew I was up for it, and it got me thinking back to the days of kicking a ball without shoes and socks on the fields at home in Penylan, Swansea when I was about 15 years old. I've never kicked better or further than I did then! But this kick went OK and straight through the posts from about 50 yards. In fact, I was so thrilled I jumped into the air and straight into Tommy David's arms! I'd never done anything like that before, or since!

Hefin Jenkins – Number 8

22, 6' 4", 16st., one of Llanelli's finest discoveries and a forward of tremendous potential – a triple international at rugby, Junior Schoolboy, Secondary Schoolboy, and Youth – Welsh Senior Trials; also an athletics international at schoolboy level, trainee valuer

I can remember clearly that wherever we went along either touchline, it was as if the noise was following us round all the time. In any other game, it would come and go, but not that day. I don't remember a great deal of detail at all, it was all lost on the cut and thrust of the game itself.

The line-outs were certainly central, with Delme playing a key role. We couldn't lift the players in those days, of course – we had to jump off our own steam. But it was possible, shall we say, to prop up the player who was jumping sometimes – what we could call steadying them, by putting our shoulder under their backside when they were in the air. We could always protect the one jumping by keeping the opposition away from him. We varied the line-out positions on their throw and ours as well. Carwyn had instilled in us that they were great going forward, so we needed to turn them at every possible opportunity. They didn't like that. This meant they had to be thinking all the time and it made them more tired.

I think we were better than them on the day, and we had two incidents which I remember kept us in the game. There was a race and a jump for the ball over the line between J.J. and Duncan Hales. J.J. won and it was no try to them. It could have been so different when Bryan Williams put a huge kick up which fell right under our posts, but Roger Davies caught it and another try was avoided. But apart from that, we felt we had things in control. But I didn't start to think we could win until it got to 9–3.

Gareth Jenkins – Flanker
21, 6' 1", 13st. 10lbs. Skipper of Llanelli and Welsh Youth teams, a player with great potential – a natural ball player who runs like a three-quarter, boilermaker

From the kick-off it was just brutal! If anyone was on the floor you knew you were going to be booted. My shirt got ripped, my ankles got done, my back got done and my head got done. They were uncompromising in their intimidation. Round and round in my head I kept saying to myself they want us to crack, they want us to crack. It was, in effect, a negative approach to the game, from us as well in the end. We just wanted to break up their play, not to stop them scoring tries, but just to stop them playing.

There was a strong sense between us on the team that we weren't going to let them have their way. We would do whatever it took. Man to man we were all mentally comfortable in that war zone.

The one incident that I won't forget was when Batty kicked into our corner at the end. He went whizzing past me. I have no idea how Benny got out of that corner and sent the ball flying up the field, seemingly kicking it over his shoulder. But it was a magnificent sight for the rest of us! That's when I knew we had won.

Tom David – Flanker

24, 6' 0", 15st., has the speed of a three-quarter and the build of a
front row forward, captained Wales 'B' this season against France 'B'
capped previously twice at 'B' level against France and Canada, and
for Welsh XV against Canada, also for Wales under-25 against Fiji,
tipped to gain senior international honours this season; native of
Pontypridd, by profession a fitter with BAOC

To be honest, I was very nervous and it was so easy to get
distracted by the crowd, the tension, the cameras, everything.
Once the game kicked-off, the nerves went. Especially of course
when Roy got the try, that eased it a bit more, but we knew we
couldn't relax. It was a battle-royal from the word go, but we
had the crowd with us. They played as much a part in that
victory as we did on the pitch.

As far as us players were concerned, we were all together.
It wasn't the prettiest of games – New Zealand made sure of
that. We fought for every ball basically, and often literally.
The one incident I can remember so clearly is Benny catching
the ball in the corner and kicking it back up field, easing the
pressure.

When the whistle went, it was like I imagine it would be
to win the Lottery now. The relief was massive, as well as the
exhilaration.

Derek Quinnell – Lock

23, 6' 3¼", 16st. 2lbs. Welsh international and British Lion, toured
Australia and New Zealand, Welsh Youth international, a player with
great courage, always found where the game is hardest – the best
has yet to be seen of this player, electrician

For all the physicality, and there was plenty of that of course,
there was a lot of psychology too. That showed itself in
various ways. The line-outs were central for us because it
was somewhere we could get at their inside backs and stop
them getting the ball wide. Mervyn Davies played a brilliant
role in that aspect on the Lions tour of 1971. I had seen
that when playing with him out there. Delme was our main

line-out forward and I was to look after him in any way I could. I moved position in the line-out throughout the game, sometimes at the back, sometimes at the front.

I had played against their captain Ian Kirkpatrick before, as well. He was a very special player, especially with ball in hand. And keeping him out of the game was a main objective too.

Psychology meant giving each of us different roles so that we could focus on what each one had to do throughout the team, but obviously I was more aware of that amongst the forwards. We were all made to feel important because we had a role to fulfil on the pitch. It wasn't a nice place to be, but it was an exciting place to be.

Delme Thomas – Lock
30, 6' 3", 16 st. 2 lbs, nineteen Welsh caps, Llanelli's most experienced international – British Lions, Wales, and Baa-Baas, toured New Zealand, Australia, South Africa, and Fiji Welsh Youth International and line-out specialist; electricity linesman

The worst thing you could do against the All Blacks was to let them come at you. You've got to go out to meet them first. I had seen that in their own country in 1971. So that was crucial for us forwards from the word go. It was an attitude of 'let's hit them, let's hit them', time and time again.

A central role in that approach for us forwards was the way Benny controlled the play behind us. So his kicking out of hand was critical. I'd been very lucky to play with both Phil Bennett and Barry John, the best two outside halves ever. They could read the game in a way you don't see so often now. That day, Phil was immense, he was the star.

When Andy Hill's kick went over, I started to think that we might well win. They then had to score twice and only then did my mind start thinking about winning.

Tony Crocker – Prop

30, 6' 0", 15 st. 7lbs. The quiet man of the team; a fine worker, and a great clubman; extremely popular with everyone, engineer

The atmosphere certainly did hit me when I walked out onto the pitch first, but like some of the other boys, that whistle blowing for the kick-off concentrates your mind back on the game. For me the build-up had been that I was playing against this beast called Murdoch. He was a big lad certainly, quite intimidating in the way he looked at you. But I didn't think he was as bad as everyone made out he was. I certainly came across one or two just as bad in league games up and down south Wales! He was very hard, I have to say that, but I didn't find there was anything to fear about him.

I don't know if they were a bit raw, being the second game of the tour, but they had played well enough at Gloucester. In the second half we showed a lot of courage to hold out and keep the lead we got in the first five minutes.

Roy Thomas – Hooker

27, 5' 11", 14 st. Capped for Wales 'B' against France, reserve for Wales on numerous occasions, one of the finest hookers in the game; steelworker

I remember that it was pressure all the time because they just didn't let up. It was all the time, a knee on your elbow, a hand holding you down, and on and on. Not much of it would get noticed, but it was there from beginning to end. Keith Murdoch ended up stepping on my head at one point. I'm not sure if he did it deliberately, but he drew blood from me with his studs, without doubt. The problem was that only put more fire into me! I just couldn't wait to get to the next scrum and rip him apart.

We had that great early lead, which made a difference of course, and keeping it tight from then on was what it was all about. Right towards the end we had a scrum; the ball came out and, as we were beginning to run up field, the ref blew. We'd won! I had beaten Australia when I played for Swansea as a youngster. That was obviously special. But when that whistle went and we had beaten the All Blacks – that meant more, because New Zealand was the team who beat all who went in front of them. But we had beaten them this time!

Barry Llewelyn – Prop
24, 6' 2½", 16 st. 4lbs, 12 Welsh caps, toured Australia with Welsh party in 1969, outstanding forward and Llanelli skipper, product of star Llanelli Grammar School rugby team; schoolmaster

My recall of matches is usually very poor because most of the time I'm looking at the grass. But I remember bits of this one! What a marvellous start we had with that try from Budgie! Strangely, I remember something from right at the end of the game. We'd been in a ruck or a maul or something and play was moving on. I was getting up onto my hands and knees and I felt an almighty kick right up my backside, which flattened me. It was Mr Murdoch's foot that was responsible. The ref came up to me as I was lying there, because it really hurt, and told me off for wasting time at the end of the game! There was even blood on my shorts!

If we had an attacking line-out on the 25, I was to stand out at outside half, ready to take the ball in the burst. There was a chance to do just that towards the end of the game, when we knew we had to keep things tight. But I took up position for an attacking line-out on the 25 at outside half. As I went to do so, automatically almost, I could hear Phil shouting at me 'No, no, don't do it!' He was afraid that if I spilled the ball they could be away. Luckily nothing came of it!

I was in the Newport team that beat South Africa as well, in 1969, so I then had the New Zealand scalp. The reaction to the South Africa victory was not as euphoric as it was on the day we beat the All Blacks in Llanelli.

iii Enjoying the victory

When that final whistle went, it was pandemonium! The field, in an instant, was invaded by as many fans as could get onto a blade of grass. The players were mobbed; Delme lifted high in the air and carried proudly on tired, ecstatic shoulders above a sea of people swarming around him. That image has become the iconic symbol of that victory. It was, however, to be misunderstood by some elements of the press. But not the Welsh press, of course. Some saw the clenched fist gesture as an intimidating response which carried the celebrations too far. Whoever wrote that just didn't get it. In replying to those comments, veteran New Zealand rugby journalist Terry McLean had an answer for his fellow writers. 'But did they not understand, these critics, that Delme and Carwyn and all of the Welsh were brothers under the skin. That, having lived so much in the misery of mining and associated crafts, they had come to believe they could, if they tried, conquer the world? Which right now, they had done.'

Terry McLean got it. He rounds up his reply to the critics with a sentence loftier than Delme himself ever was on that day. 'Delme Thomas was not a man riding upon shoulders. He was the archangel of Cambria.' Not many a rugby player over decades of world rugby, has been called an archangel, especially by a journalist from the country his team had just beaten!

'When the match was over,' try-scoring hero Roy Bergiers remembers, 'I went to shake hands with their two centres, Robertson and Sayers, and then in an instant we were engulfed by the fans. Some friends from Carmarthen wanted to carry me on their shoulders, but got it wrong and I ended up top half of me on the floor and my leg in the air! I felt shy and overwhelmed by the whole thing to be honest.'

But, before getting to the dressing room, Roy managed to do one specific thing. 'At the end of every game, Ken Jones, the secretary, would collect the match balls, two of them usually, and put them back in the filing cabinet in his office. I saw him do this that day and asked him if I could keep one of them. He gave me one thankfully, and I then went round every one of the players from both teams, in the course of the evening, getting their signatures on it. It was a Gilbert match ball, and any subsequent one that's come to light in recent years can't be the actual one – I treasure that ball very much to this day!'

Roy does say, however, that he had a great deal of difficulty in getting two or three of the All Blacks to sign the ball. Two of their hardcore inner circle only agreed to do so when he went back to them for a third time of asking.

The players took an age to get off the pitch that day, much to the frustration of the All Blacks. Keen to get to the refuge of the dressing room as soon as possible, they found every route blocked by ecstatic fans. That, no doubt, added insult to injury.

'Once we managed to get back to the dressing room, that was jam-packed too! The fans were in there and through all the corridors around,' recalls Roger Davies. 'Grown men were hugging each other; lots of the boys who had taken their kits off were standing there naked, being hugged by fans and committee men alike! The guy who was my best man found his way in somehow. It was extremely emotional! There was one chap at Stradey whose job it was to make tea for the teams after each game. He obviously thought that that day should be no exception. I remember seeing him walking down the corridor towards the away team changing rooms, carrying a big tray best he could, full of mugs and a giant teapot. The All Blacks dressing room door must have been ajar and, having no hands free, he pushed it open with his foot to carry the tea in to them. It was obviously met by a solid foot from the other side which closed the door in his face, sending the poor man sprawling back against the corridor wall, tea and crockery flying everywhere! He definitely got the impression that they didn't want a cup of tea!'

In the mayhem under the stands, there were even stories of fans taking mud from the boots and socks of the players. 'It was being on a high and it was being in a state of shock at the same time' is what Andy Hill recalls. Most players held on to their jerseys, all except one.

'I had been given a shirt after the South Africa tour by Mike Trueman,' Hefin Jenkins recalls. 'He had a shirt from the Transvaal team I wanted, because I collected shirts. Most of them are at Burry Port Rugby Club now. When he gave it to me, Mike said that he'd like my jersey after the All Blacks game in return. So that's what I had to do and he was obviously very pleased indeed! I've no idea where it is now, and Mike passed away a while ago.'

But, after what seemed like an age, the crowd dispersed, and a little order was restored, albeit temporarily. There was a reception buffet for both squads in the patrons' bar immediately after the game. Gareth Jenkins was given some rather unusual advice. 'I came off the pitch with two lovely black eyes. A guy came up to me in the reception, smoking a pipe. He enthused about the game and said how well we'd done and the rest of it. Then he referred to my black eyes, saying he was used to that because he used to do a bit of boxing himself. He was from London originally, but was living in Gorseinon, near Swansea at the time. Then he told me that the only answer to black eyes was to put meat steaks on them – they were guaranteed to heal them quickly and properly. Oh thank you for that I said, knowing that there was a fat chance of me buying steaks to put on my eyes! With that, he put something in my blazer top pocket, told me it was for the steaks and walked off. I took it out to see – it was a £10 note! At that time I was earning about £23 a week. He's just given me half a week salary almost to buy meat to put on my eyes! So, needless to say, I didn't buy steaks with it but used it instead to cover my wages for the following day so that I could take a day off after celebrating. That guy paid for my day off!'

The players were quickly turning into heroes and, as Tommy David says, it was a day when you never had to put your hand in your pocket. After the reception buffet, there was a lull – of sorts – for the players to get ready for the evening functions, the highlight of which was the Rugger Ball at the town's Glen Ballroom at 8 p.m. The Glen was the entertainment centre for Llanelli, attracting top bands too throughout that decade, from Mud to Showaddywaddy. That evening though, it was to host a unique event.

Some players went home to change, to collect their wives or girlfriends, but there was to be no peace wherever they went. It was something that they'd have to get used to. The rest of that season would not be the same, the next few years of their playing careers would not be the same and indeed, they still carry that badge of beating the All Blacks to this day.

Gareth Jenkins walked home from Stradey to the neighbouring village of Furnace, where he lived next door to the Colliers' pub. The village itself was named after a furnace which made cannonballs for other famous victories, such as Trafalgar. 'I couldn't get near the house; the whole square was full of people and cars on stop, unable to get through. It was unreal.'

'I called in at my parents' home in that gap,' says Phil, 'and on the way, I saw about six policemen playing touch rugby with one of their helmets on the side of the road! Then, I went in to see my father, which was a special moment. He couldn't come to see me play, and my mum was always too nervous to watch me, so going there then meant a lot, you couldn't buy that. Of course, as soon as word got out that I was there, everyone in the street was there as well!'

In the toilets of the Glen Ballroom, J.J. remembers a confrontation with some All Blacks. 'Tommy and I had gone to the gents, and Sid Going came in and stood next to me. He was one of their legends, of course, even though he didn't play that day. I just turned to him and said something along the lines of "Bad luck today" in hopefully a polite way. He turned to me, said, "F*** off!" and walked straight out! We were slightly taken aback by that, but then I have wondered since how I would have reacted if someone did the same to me in similar circumstances. I hope I would take it in the spirit I meant it that day, but who knows!'

The entertainment laid on for the players that evening was none other than Wales' foremost duo, Ryan and Ronnie. Both Hefin Jenkins and Roy Bergiers remember that clearly, although the rest aren't quite so clear on that detail! The duo, who would go on to dominate entertainment in both languages throughout that decade, were at the start of their careers then, at least, they were at the start of their English-language career.

It was only just a year before the All Blacks game that Ryan and Ronnie had decided to try their hand at English-language light entertainment routines. Their unique brand of singing and sketches had been hugely successful in Welsh before then. But 1971 saw them venture to perform to English audiences. Everyone wanted to know whether their brand of humour would translate. Their appearances in clubs throughout Wales would have been a part of the transition process. In the same year, Ryan was cast in a main role alongside Richard Burton, Elizabeth Taylor and Peter O'Toole in the classic film version of Dylan Thomas' *Under Milk Wood*.

'They used to come to Llanelli RFC's social club,' Les Williams recalls. 'I used to help out on the doors then and, whenever they were with us, they would give me a few LPs, on vinyl, to say thank you for helping out on the night. These had songs they'd just recorded or something like that on them. I only wish I'd kept them now!'

Ryan and Ronnie went on to become household names on television and at live venues throughout Wales and beyond, with their Christmas pantomime at the Grand Theatre, Swansea, becoming a national institution. But that October evening in 1972, they sang and performed their sketches to a ballroom full of people who were too delirious to notice what else was going on!

After the Glen celebrations, the team headed back to the Ashburnham Hotel to continue the merriment. Some, however, chose to go home for a variety of reasons. Roger Davies had a prior engagement! 'We had promised to go out with some friends to a do at the Uplands Rugby Club. It was probably something to do with Halloween, I would imagine. We never used to go there and have probably never been since, but we'd arranged that night and we kept to our plans. The reception in the club when we got there was fantastic, I must say. There was plenty of cheering, talking, and questioning all night. It was great. We had planned to go back to join the boys later in the night, but we took so long to get out of town to go to the Uplands, we were late getting there, and we would have taken an age to get back to Llanelli as well, so we didn't try. Before going there though, I made one call which turned out to be a very special one for me. I went to see my parents. My dad is a very placid man, doesn't show much emotion – even when watching a game on TV or something he wouldn't get excited at all. When I went into the house, he was really emotional. That hit me and I can't think too much about it today, because it gets me going again.'

Andy Hill had gone home fairly early too, feeling too emotionally drained after three or four pints, to carry on. But that was no trouble for most of them, the indefatigable Shanto, in particular. 'It took me ages before I would say this story, but I think it's safe now! I had driven to the Ashburnham from Penclawdd. So how was I going to get back after a few shandies? It was by then close on half four in the morning. A policeman was at the Ash – can't remember why he was there – checking everything was OK, I presume. He asked me how I was getting home. I didn't have much of an answer and he said, "OK, Roy, jump in your car." I did, and next thing there was a police car in front of me, me in the middle and the policeman who spoke to me in a car behind. We went in convoy like that all the way to the border with Glamorgan, as it was then, which was the Loughor bridge. I was told to go across the bridge on my own, and on the other side two more police cars were waiting to take me from there home to Penclawdd! I had two police escorts that day, but that last one was probably a little more unique than the first!'

For their part, the New Zealand team had been back at the Dragon Hotel in Swansea for some time. They spent the evening enjoying the Swansea nightlife at the famous Townsman nightclub. One newspaper reporter, Joanna Kilmartin of the *Observer*, tracked them down. 'Later that evening in Swansea we all went to the Townsman's disco. The impact of so much masculinity (the side rates high on good looks) was instantaneous, as it has been everywhere. (If the girls swarm too close, Kirkpatrick has only to nod his head and the players melt away.) After such a beating, it was surprising they were prepared to let their hair down, drinking deeply and listening to the local cabaret (sample joke: In Belfast there are only 40 shops to go until Christmas).'

Obviously things had mellowed a little in the All Blacks camp by then. That would soon change again of course, once the newspaper reports hit the newsstands on Wednesday morning. Today, Bryan Williams sees the game with a distinct clarity. 'The one thing that stood out was the passion and intensity of the Llanelli team, but also the passion and intensity of the crowd. That hit us hard. We couldn't believe that the crowd were so close to us, thousands and thousands within touching distance, baying for our blood! When Bergiers got that try, the momentum shifted on the pitch straightaway. Comment was made – I think by Carwyn James as well – that we didn't seem to have a Plan B. In the face of such momentum I don't think it would make any difference if we had a Plan B or a Plan C. I had to go off, having taken a whack on the thigh with about 20 minutes left and I walked off feeling sorry for myself, knowing we were behind and up against it. Basically, from our point of view, immaturity and bad management contributed to our loss. At the end we were hurting, no doubt. But we also knew we were beaten by a better side. What made quite an impression was seeing what the victory meant to the people of Llanelli. I didn't like where we were as a team at that moment at all, but it was plain even for us to see that the whole town was shaken by that win, and that it went deep with the fans around us. That was quite something to see.'

As an aside to Bryan Williams' presence on the pitch that day, the now president of the NZRU shared the experience with a player who would become chairman of the WRU. The curtain raiser for the match was Llanelli under-12s versus Neath under-12s. Llanelli lost 4–0 and the game's only score, a try, was scored by a certain D. Pickering, as the team photo shows. David Pickering would go on to play for Llanelli and Wales.

For many of the Llanelli boys, it was back to work on that Wednesday after the game. Captain Delme Thomas was one of them. 'I've never been one for drinking and I didn't that night. But that wasn't the point. It was as if no one wanted to go, to leave the atmosphere, the occasion. I got home about three in the morning, I think, and I was in work by eight. Everyone there was looking daft at me and wondering why I had turned up. Well, that was my work at the end of the day. I wouldn't think of not going in.'

Roy Bergiers was standing in a classroom teaching children that morning, as was Barry Llewelyn, but J.J. was on his unofficial day off. Andy Hill had Scarlet fever that day too and didn't show for work. Prop forward Tony Crocker was back at Morris Motors, but with a little difference. 'It felt as if I went straight back to work from the Ash to be honest! When I got in the manager came up to me straight away, before I was in properly and, after a chat about the game, told me he was changing my duties for the day. I was to be outside in the grounds instead of in the factory. When I asked why, the answer was simple. If I did work inside, he said, it would stop production completely as everyone would want to talk to me. Everyone, that is, who were in a state to turn up for work themselves after the day before!'

A week later, Morris Motors held a big party for Tony at the works social club to honour the achievement of one of their own.

That again was something the players would have to get used to. There were functions of all sorts ahead of them. Centenary functions were already organised, of course. Now, there would be victory functions to add to them through the club itself, but also through a myriad of societies and organisations who wanted to do their bit to mark the Scarlets achievement.

So for all the history that had led up to 31 October 1972, this was very much the team of the club's finest hour. They had created a new piece of their own history. It was their moment.

8

The fans' game

Rugby is a wonderful show:
dance, opera and suddenly the blood of killing!

Richard Burton, film star and frustrated rugby player

THEY WERE HEROES. They were giants. Two headline phrases
used by the *Western Mail* newspaper in the match report the
day after the victory. But they weren't heroes and giants in
isolation of course, nor in their own eyes, either. They were
so in the eyes of others: the fans. Bryan Williams has already
credited the passion and intensity of the fans as a major factor
in their defeat. The impact that victory created would be felt
for years to come.

Amongst the pack of journalists at Stradey that day, was the
much-respected Clem Thomas, from the *Observer*. Clem played
for Swansea, captained Wales nine times in the 1950s and was
a British Lion, but is perhaps best remembered for supplying
the famous cross kick for Ken Jones to score the winning try
for Wales against the All Blacks – the last time Wales beat them
in 1953. He was a butcher by trade, but turned to journalism,
working for the *Observer* for over 35 years. In a piece in the
newspaper after the game, he sums up the fans' contribution.
'There is at Stradey Park an intensity of parochial feeling,
love of the game, and enthusiasm far beyond anything I have
experienced anywhere in the rugby world. Not even in other
parts of Wales, South Africa, Fiji or even Otago, New Zealand,
have I experienced such vehemently violent passion and it is

the only place I know where the crowd leads the pack and often referees the match as well.'

As the knowledge that their club had just beaten the All Blacks began to sink in, the delirious fans' first move after the celebrations at Stradey was to hit the town's pubs, many of them charging past New Zealand Street on their way to the nearest pub, The White Horse. It was this pub, so legend has it, which ran out of beer first on that day when, famously, the pubs ran dry. Later on, The White Horse would be owned by Norman Gale, but by now its doors have closed for good.

Match reports fail to establish how many fans were actually at the game. Press stories quote figures ranging from 18,000 to 27,000. Added to that, of course, are the stories told by people over the years, claiming to be there themselves, so the total attendance is probably greater than the population of the Llanelli region and more than double the capacity of Stradey.

As it was, the number in the ground was over half the population of the town at the time. It's probably still impossible to know exactly how many were there, but committee man, Marlston Morgan, who was the man responsible for the ticketing, has a clearer idea than most. 'I would say 25,000 people were there. We were lucky to have had the South Africa game in January 1970, so we had something to work from. But the demand for this game was far greater. For us as a club, right from the word go, school children were a main target and we made sure as many as possible could get in. I don't think there was an official day off for schools, but the education authority gave each headmaster the right to decide for their own school. I was responsible for getting the pop crates and the timbers for the children to sit on around the ground.'

It was an all-ticket game, but Llanelli were not to benefit financially at all from ticket sales. Being an official tour, it was a Welsh Rugby Union fixture and, as such, all proceeds went to them. 'All we had was the takings from the bar and the car park, which of course on a day like that, were substantial enough. But no ticket money, not even a percentage.'

However many were actually there, everyone has their own story – each one central and special to their enjoyment of the whole experience. Many are quite simply not true however, including some told while researching for this book. One policeman said he'd got home soaked to the skin after standing outside on duty all day. But, it didn't rain. And that gentleman in a Llanelli pub who waxed lyrical about the occasion, spoilt it all when he went on and on about the score being 9–6 and made it worse for himself when he wouldn't be told otherwise. There were other similar tales. But feeling the need to say such stories, with a certain degree of pride all these years later, shows a definite desire for some kind of ownership of the event, even if the facts were wrong.

There are stories, of course, which are an integral part of the waft and weave of that day, each one unique and representative. In the *Western Mail*, one supporter, Clyde Evans, is said to have put his pint down on the pavement, 'under the benevolent gaze of a policeman' and proceeded to tell the officer that this was indeed, 'one of the greatest days in the history of Welsh rugby'. The policeman's response isn't recorded, but no doubt he had no grounds to disagree with him.

Mark Sayers was in the lower sixth form at Llanelli Boys' Grammar School in 1972. He was representative of so many others who were at the club at that time, an example of how clubs were run in those days. His father, Dai, was the ground's safety officer, a purely voluntary role, as he worked for the electricity board during the week. His mother, Jean, would help prepare the food in the kitchen after games. These links brought with them obvious benefits, for the sons usually, but often the daughters as well. Mark was with the Llanelli squad when they gathered on the Sunday afternoon at Stradey, listening to Carwyn James talk to his players. 'My father had gone along, as did some of the other people involved with the club and I just went along with him. It was a natural enough thing to do. I sat in a corner somewhere and listened to Carwyn's pep talk, quite low key at that point, but it involved a lot of analysis of the game the day before against Western Counties. One of the most bizarre things I remember him saying was telling the forwards to sharpen their studs! That made quite an impression on me! I knew most of the players anyway and they wouldn't have thought it strange at all that a schoolchild was hanging around. The following day, I went with my father to the Ashburnham Golf Club where the team had gathered the night before the game. That was very relaxed and the players just spent some time together before the big event.'

Not long after this, Mark began to referee rugby games. He still does, and is now president of the Welsh Referees' Society. On the match day itself, he had specific responsibilities. 'I was in the scoreboard that day, as I had been for a couple of seasons by 1972. There were three of us in there usually. One by the 'Goals' window, one by the 'Tries' and one by the 'Points', just under the name Llanelli! The scoreboard hadn't been there that long, there wouldn't have been one at all throughout most of the 1960s, and it was one of the innovations brought in by the committee. They did put in a little perspex window in the top right hand corner for us to see out of, but it was no good at all – too high up and no good for three of us! So we looked through the gaps either side of the numbers.'

Alongside him were friends Caerwyn Owen and David Challenor. 'I think that might have been my first year in the scoreboard,' says David. 'The ritual was pretty much the same that day as any other. Firstly, we had to go under the stand to get a ten-foot ladder and carry it out onto the pitch, along the length of the main stand and up the bank under the scoreboard.'

'We would then place the ladder in line with the trap-door in the floor of the scoreboard, high above us,' continues Caerwyn Owen, 'and place the ladder up to it. Then, one by one, climb up into the scoreboard. What often used to happen, of course, is that once we were in there, with the ladder pulled in behind us, some fan would lift a child on his shoulders to lock the trap door from the outside! At the end of games, we would have to stick our heads out of one of the small windows and plead to be let out!'

Before the game, when the All Blacks went out to the side of the pitch, many of them noticed the scoreboard and the name of their team in a strange language. Those fans close to them under the stand said that this caused some discussion amongst them: the name of their team in a language they didn't understand seen as one further piece of intimidation, of making them feel uncomfortable. For the scoreboard boys, the pre-match routine was very similar to any other game, even though they went through it a lot earlier, fighting their way through the crowd with a ten-foot ladder. 'I think we had more match nerves that day, despite the obvious passion and intensity of the crowd,' says David. 'We were more worried about whether Llanelli were going to win or not than whether we would make a mistake. We were fans at the end of the day.'

Not long before that game, tries were worth three points. In order to help the scorers, a sign had been stuck on the inside scoreboard wall saying, 'Tries are now worth four points'. Every little helps. A converted try would be put down under Goal, an unconverted one under Try. 'I was lucky,' says Caerwyn. 'I was usually on the Points window, which would be the first one to fill up after getting into double figures, leaving no room for me to look out! It was up to the other two then! The scores for the visiting team were right down by our feet.'

'We couldn't have been in a better position for the Llanelli try as it was right in front of us – lucky on a day like that!' Mark adds, 'We could so easily have turned away after the penalty hit the crossbar, to put the number three back down or something, but we didn't and we saw everything clearly.'

At the end of the game, they can't remember if anyone had tried to lock them in the scoreboard that day. Once out, they made their way back, with a ten-foot ladder as a weapon, through and under the stands to see the mayhem and jubilation there for themselves. 'Usually after games we would go to the players' lounge, and help clear the glasses up or whatever and then we'd have a meal at the end ourselves. It wasn't quite like that that day recalled Caerwyn.

'I clearly remember Grav,' Mark adds, 'coming up to me full of excitement, shouting and cheering in the weights room under the stand. "Marky! Marky!" he shouted at me as he embraced me, "I sorted Mark Sayers out today!" A reference to the fact that the All Black number 12 that day was also called Mark Sayers!' And being under the stand after the game paid off for Llanelli's Mark Sayers, as he managed to get his match programme autographed by the All Blacks team.

As Marlston Morgan said, the club had specifically targeted school children to be a part of the big occasion. Hundreds marched from their respective schools from all points around the town. Craig Williams remembers walking from Stebonheath School at the opposite end of town to Stradey – there were hundreds of children in convoy for the three miles to the ground. The same story would have been true of Stradey, Coleshill, Girls' Grammar and Boys' Grammar Schools.

Mark Sayers' brother, Andrew, saw the game sat on concrete steps in the stand, next to his father in the committee box. The day after the game, Mark was still off school and went back to Stradey to see who was still around, just to squeeze as many more drops of emotion as possible out of the occasion. He wasn't alone.

On leaving the ground after the match, many fans had just about enough time to collect their winnings from the bets they'd placed, although there weren't many of them. Very few backed Llanelli to win, at least by showing the colour of their money. One fan is said to have earned £12 after 12–1 odds in favour of Llanelli, and a man who lost £1 joyfully declared that he had never been so happy to lose money!

The after-match feeling was one of frustration for former player, then committee man, Marlston Morgan. 'As a former player, who'd faced the All Blacks myself, I could really appreciate what had just happened and wanted to enjoy it with the team. But, I had my official duties to attend to. As well as the ticketing, I was also responsible for the press that day, so I was really busy after the game and couldn't get involved for far too long with the festivities!'

The British media, along with those who were there with New Zealand, were accommodated in a temporary press room, set up in the building right next to the Stradey entrance. That's where Welsh Water had their offices, and their works canteen was turned into a rugby press centre. Marlston adds, 'There were some sandwiches laid on for them there and tea, of course, as well as phones for reports to be phoned through. I was running back and forth from there to fetch various players that the reporters wanted to talk to and, as I was doing so, having to dip in and out of the celebrations. I was one of them and wanted to be with them, but I had to wait a little while.'

Doubtless no one walked more that day than Alan T. Richards. He worked at Trostre tinplate works and had done so since the early 1950s, not long after the works opened. By 1972, photography was a hobby of growing importance to Alan and one which he'd started to use at his workplace. If ever there's a story that shows the lengths some had to go to, to show their passion for a club, it's Alan's. He wasn't so much a volunteer – he did get paid for his work – but he was, in reality, enjoying his hobby when he went down to Stradey, come rain or shine, to take photographs of the matches. The All Blacks game was no exception. Having secured time off work to go down to the game, he headed for Stradey.

'The radio bulletins in the car on the way from Trostre to Stradey were full of reports of traffic queues and saying where we could or couldn't park. So I parked a little way from the ground and walked the rest of the way. I walked more than anyone else during games themselves because I never liked staying in one place. In any one match I would probably walk round the pitch about five or six times and face a barrage of banter from fans telling me to move out of their way! But it was friendly enough, thank goodness.'

Alan Richards began to use his interest in photography at

his workplace, being called upon to take photographs of any accidents or incidents at the plant for the company's records. In one case, he had to photograph the scene of a particularly nasty fatal accident at Trostre. This piecemeal work led to contact with the local newspaper, *The Llanelli Star*, and an offer to take some photographs of Llanelli rugby matches. He worked on a freelance basis supplying photos to local papers from 1965 until 1988, getting paid for every photo the papers used. 'There were about twenty to thirty photographers there that day, but I just carried on doing what I always did for every game. Except, of course, there were a lot more people there for me to get in their way and a lot more to shout at me! The first big action to photo was that first penalty. I decided to position myself behind the posts, so that I could see Phil Bennett face-on in the distance, between the posts, and there would be a line of All Blacks with their backs to me in the foreground. Before Benny could take the kick, there was an injury to be attended to. In that stoppage time, I changed my mind and raced along the dead ball line, down the touchline in front of the stand and positioned myself behind Benny. From that angle, I would see the ball in flight towards the posts from the kicker's point of view. Great, that worked well.

'Except of course that the kick didn't go over and that charge down try was scored – yes, right where I was positioned originally! I would have had *the* photo of the ball being grounded, face-on and the ecstatic Scarlets behind jumping for joy. That was certainly one that got away and it's still frustrating to this day. Why on the earth did I move?' One shot Alan Richards did get, however, and a rare one it was too, was the one-off celebration of Andy Hill jumping into Tommy David's arms!

Once Alan got home, it was time to get those photos developed. This operation is well worth recounting in full, as it was complex and implausible enough to give Heath Robinson a run for his money. It also shows dedication that would please an Olympic athlete. 'When I got home after the game, the first thing I did was go upstairs to the bedroom and get under the bed clothes. That's where I would take the film out of the camera and put it into the tank I would use for developing. The bed clothes were heavy enough to make it completely dark under there. Then, downstairs to the kitchen to wash the film under the tap. I would blackout the windows and my wife and the two boys would have to sit in the living room, next to the kitchen, with only a table lamp on, as the main light would spill under the door into the kitchen and spoil the photos. For the same reason, they weren't allowed to go to the kitchen, either. The biggest light problem though was the occasional car headlamps at the back of the house. They would shine in now and again and I would have to rush to put extra covering or something between the light and the film which was developing.

'The film would be hanging up by pegs all round the kitchen then, attached to various units and whatever else was to hand. While they were drying, that's when I would have my food, in the kitchen in the dark on my own. The next step was to start making the prints. These were then put out flat all over the living room floor, about 30 or 40 of them, and left to dry until the next morning. Once they were put there, I would get my typewriter out and type captions for every single photo and then on the kitchen table cut them into thin little strips and stick them on the back of the photos when they were ready.'

The following day, during his lunch break at Trostre, Alan would drop off the prints at the newspaper office in Llanelli. The day of the All Blacks game, however, posed an extra problem. 'It was such a grey miserable day and the light was terrible. I was concerned in the car on the way home that I might not have any pictures at all in the camera, because they wouldn't come out properly due to the lack of light. Once home, I tried something different to compensate for the lack of light. Part of the developing process was to put the film in liquid and bring the temperature up. Let's say I used to set the temperature at 68 degrees, that day I increased it to about 75 but left it on that heat for a little less time, in the hope of getting a little extra from the process. I ran the risk, of course, of losing everything anyway by making it too hot for the film, but luckily it worked just right and it lifted the images just enough.'

Thanks to such dedication and that little bit of extra know-how, Alan's photographs are to this day a valuable record of that historic event. He still gets calls from people asking for copies of his prints, with family members wanting records of their parents or grandparents seen in the crowd shots, or the rugby fan wanting his or her memento of the day.

A trainee reporter at the *Llanelli Star* should not have been at the game, but he was. Barrie Thomas had not long arrived at the paper after working for various local companies in the town. He recalls the old-fashioned newspaper office feel to the place, with the big printing press in a room behind the office and his desk next to an open coal fire. Unexpectedly, he was given a chance to go to Stradey.

'There were two newspaper giants in Llanelli, brothers Harry and Wilf Davies. Harry was for years called Harry Scarlet, which he would write under the Llanelli match day programme, amongst other things. Wilf was a freelance journalist, who would supply many Fleet Street agencies with copy. He got me into the match, as a runner for him, despite the fact that I wouldn't have been allowed to go for my own paper. I didn't have a seat; I stood right at the back of the stand, behind the press. Wilf was down the front writing his report. Every ten minutes or so, he would call me down, hand me a piece of paper, and I would run as fast as I could out of the stand, down the stairs to the foyer of the club, where there was a phone. That's where I would phone through to Fleet Street what Wilf had written.'

Barrie would go on to become the sports editor of the *Llanelli Star* within a couple of years, and he has published some of his Llanelli sporting stories in a book. There was another advantage of being where he was for the game too. 'Because I was back and forth, with no seat, when the game ended I was right in Carwyn James' path when he got up to leave his seat. As he came past me, I extended my hand to him and said "Llongyfarchiadau Carwyn!" I was the first to do so, I'm sure!'

Rugby had traditionally been a man's sport – certainly at that time only men would play the game. It was, however, slowly becoming much more of a mixed spectator sport. Any crowd shot, taken by Alan Richards or any other photographer, would show a predominantly male crowd. But there were exceptions, certainly in the stand, but also on that bastion of male dominance, Tanner Bank. 'I absolutely loved rugby,' says Ellen Lloyd, a Llanelli girl who at that time was a student in Cardiff. 'I would live and breathe it. But unfortunately, lots of my friends would rather go tenpin bowling or something. But I would still go to Stradey, weekends and midweek, wearing the sheepskin coat my mother bought me from the catalogue to keep warm. I was there on my own to watch the All Blacks, standing on the Tanner Bank amongst the crowd. But even as a woman there alone, in such a crowd, there was no way that I felt intimidated. They'd always look out for me, fair play, and ask someone to curb the language because "there was a lady present"! There was always a feeling of togetherness and it was a lot more noticeable that day. It was obvious when we walked to the ground. I can only describe it like being an army and the whole town had been immobilised, marching as to war and feeling a bit like the Charge of the Light Brigade marching into the Valley of Death! Our little poor industrial town was taking on the might of the All Blacks. That was an inclusive feeling too. As a woman I was there in the minority, but it was a total mix of all sorts of backgrounds together anyway, flat caps and sheepskin coats. The feeling after the win stayed for months and months, after.'

On the other side to the Tanner Bank, another ardent Scarlet fan stood not six feet away from the players' tunnel. 'The first big impression made on me that day was seeing people walking to the ground from all directions,' remembers Llangennech-born fan, Cenwyn Edwards, 'and the band walking in from the centre of Llanelli town, giving the streets all around quite a unique atmosphere. There was a strong feeling of a constant build-up for a long time before the game, which involved the whole town.'

Standing next to Cenwyn Edwards was one of the stars of Welsh rugby in the 1960s. Cenwyn had just started working on HTV's new news magazine programme, *Y Dydd*, and he subsequently went on to be head of current affairs at HTV, then a commissioning editor with S4C before being the channel's head of co-productions. He is now a media consultant. Standing next to him at Stradey in '72 was a colleague from HTV, former Wales and British Lion winger, Dewi Bebb, who was also one of the early presenters of *Y Dydd*.

Dewi Bebb was a clinical left wing, who played his club rugby for Swansea. First capped for Wales in 1959, he scored 11 tries for his country in 34 internationals. He was on the same British and Irish Lions tour to Australia and New Zealand as Delme Thomas in 1966 and he played in the same Wales team as Llanelli's assistant coach that day, Norman Gale. Dewi Bebb passed away in 1996 following a very successful second career in broadcasting, notably through HTV's ever popular *Sports Arena* which he edited, and the coverage of the first two rugby World Cups in 1987 and 1991.

'It was Norman who got the tickets for Dewi and myself,' explains Cenwyn. 'He wasn't a Llanelli fan at all, but he wanted to see the team play the All Blacks. He had played at Stradey many a time, and he obviously knew the pitch very well, judging by the comments he made about where the slope was to our left and so on. After Andy Hill's penalty, I remember him turning to me and saying, "They're going to win this you know!" It's not the kind of thing I would expect Dewi to say at all. He wasn't an excitable person who made many rash comments about anything, but he really felt that Llanelli had it in them to win.'

At the end of the game, with Dewi Bebb proved correct, Cenwyn Edwards remembers one thing clearly. 'No one knew where to go or what to do! It was a strange feeling of being ecstatic but not quite sure what to do about it; there was a strong element of surprise and amazement. It was a sort of what do we do next feeling. People who lived in the houses between Stradey and the town came out to talk to the fans leaving the ground, and no one seemed to want the whole thing to end. People who didn't know each other were stopping for chats, sharing the excitement. There was no way I could get a bus home that night; it would take too long to get through the packed streets of Llanelli. So I walked the five miles or so back to my parents' house.'

The fans' obsession with that victory didn't end at sunset that day, of course. The euphoria was to be felt for a long time after. It led to one new sight outside the social club on match days for weeks afterwards. 'I was responsible for a table in the car park,' Les Williams explains, 'from which we would sell souvenirs of the All Blacks game. It was the run-up to Christmas, of course, and the club wanted to take advantage of that. I've no doubt, mind you, that we would have sold quite well if it was near Christmas or not, because we won. But Christmas certainly added to it. A tie was produced, with a saucepan, a fern and 9–3 on it. We had red and black pens with 9–3 on them as well. And what went well was a brass rugby ball on a plinth, recording the details of the victory. It was made by Rees Industries in Bynea, a village just outside Llanelli, and the foundry was run by former Scarlets, Wales and British Lions star, Terry Davies. On a recent programme on S4C, *Twrio* – an antiques auction programme – one of these went for £70.'

So, a foundry forges a brass memento to a victory on the rugby field. There was no keeping rugby and heavy industry apart.

One young boy observed another old tradition and showed a fair degree of opportunism at the game as well. The *Llanelli Star* tells the story and draws attention to what they claim is the only person amongst the twenty thousand plus at Stradey who could be deemed as having lost out on 31 October 1972. A young schoolboy had the initiative to go to the ground in search of a penny for the guy, ahead of Bonfire night the week after. He had, however, dressed the guy in a Scarlet jersey. The newspaper comments that he should have put an All Black jersey on it and he would have made a fortune!

The victory was noted by both fans and the club in many other ways too. Posters were sold: one, a team photo of the All Blacks squad signed by them, the other a poem written by a fan and signed by all the Llanelli players. It was an early sign of the commercialisation of rugby. If such a victory happened today, of course, the marketing campaign would be in instant full swing and reaping substantial rewards. But, ironically, it's because we are in a more commercial sporting world that such a fixture doesn't happen any more. In 1972, many people were inspired to commemorate the win in that age-old Welsh tradition of putting it to verse, both in Welsh and in English. Here are three examples:

The All Blacks' Visit – 31st October 1972

The excitement was tense, 'twas Llanelli's great test
  With crowds pouring in, north, south, east and west.
It was the Scarlet's Centenary Year,
  'Twas the game of the season, the All Blacks were here.
A game years gone by, lives in my memory,
  A game when they beat us by eight points to three.
In the days of Albert and Nepia and Finch,
  A day when the Scarlets did not yield an inch.
We are hoping today to reverse that old score,
  Maybe even add a point or two more.
Stradey was packed – no more could get in,
  Packed just as tight as sardines in a tin.
The All Blacks were heavier by over a ton,
  Which is quite a fair weight, after all's said and done.
Yet the Scarlets we felt had nothing to fear,
  For this was their Centenary Year.

At last the kick off, the crowd gives a roar,
  A roar that was heard for ten miles or more,

A roar that shook the All Blacks to the core,
They had never heard anything like it before.
Despite all their weight, our boys did not care
And from scrum after scrum they had more than their share.
Came Bergiers' great try, a try of all tries –
Tears of joy in everyone's eyes;
Except the All Blacks, now looking quite glum,
Beginning to wonder what more was to come.
Phil Bennett converted, things now did look black
For the New Zealand team as they started to crack.
At last they get a penalty goal,
Raising false hopes to get out of the hole
Though a penalty goal is all very fine,
They had no chance in hell of crossing our line.

Half time no doubt, brought them welcomed relief,
For what they'd gone through was beyond all belief.
How the crowd were enjoying each thrill and each laugh,
Enthralled by the skill of our phantom fly-half,
As the biggest All Black he just brushes aside,
Calmly clears the ball, never once kicking wide.
Now a glorious penalty kicked by young Hill;
The All Blacks looking gloomier still,
For now they knew their end was in sight,
An end brought about by the Scarlets' great fight.
There on the board was the score plain to see,
Llanelli had won by nine points to three.
So ended the game, perhaps the best ever seen,
As played by the GLORIOUS LLANELLI FIFTEEN.

Jack Symmonds

Delme

Eniller pêl neu'i cholli – yn y ryc,
    bydd braich noeth amdani,
    Doed yn uchel, mae Delme
    Lan uwch y lein i'w chael hi.

Dic Jones

St. Crispin's Day at Stradey
(In honour of Carwyn James)

Now Carwyn of Cefneithin, by St. Elli's bones he vowed
That rugby lovers everywhere of Sospan should be proud.
By St. Elli's bones he vowed it that our forwards and our backs.
Should crown our hundred glorious years by beating the All Blacks.
The tension is terrific, electrical the air,
The chanting of the multitude thrills every watcher there;
And when the players take the field, it rises to a scream
That curdles the Lliedi as it passes o'er its stream.
But Carwyn's brow is sad, and Carwyn's speech is low,
And darkly looks he at the sky, and darkly at the floor.
The rain may soon be on us. Oh, everlasting shame!
For if the ground and ball are wet, what hope to win the game!"
Then, out speaks Mighty Delme (a lion proud is he):
"Lo, who will stand at my right hand, and hold their pack with me?"
Then Hefin, Gareth, Tony, Roy, Quinnell and huge Barrie –
All shout aloud in unison, "Me, Me, Me, Me, Me, Me!"
At last the game is started, New Zealand's penalised!!
And as Phil Bennett takes the kick, the crowd is mesmerised,
And every heart beats faster, as the ball flies true and straight,
Its path is surely guided by the certain foot of Fate.
No sound of joy or sorrow is heard from the spellbound host,
The thousands gaze in dumb surprise, as it bounces off the post.
'Tis gathered up by Coiling, but big Bergiers barges through.
The crowd sends up a rap'rous cry, the deafening cheers reach the sky,
Where the peeping angels, as they lie, join in the cheering, too.
The play that followed after, and old Andy's kick so fine,
And the scenes in Sospanville that night outreach this muse of mine.
And as for Delme and his men, whom the Kiwis failed to tame,
Their memory is immortal; they're assured eternal fame.
When their grandsons romp the playground,
And their joints are stiff like mine
And their breath and steps grow shorter with the ravages of Time,
With joy and jubilation will the story still be told –
How well the Scarlets played the game, in the glorious days of old.

S. G. Rees

9

Everyone's game

I prefer rugby to soccer. I enjoy the violence in rugby,
except when they start biting each other's ears off!

Elizabeth Taylor, Hollywood goddess, 1972

UNDOUBTEDLY, THE MOST famous ode to 9–3 is the song that
bears that title, with the first line: "'Twas on a dark and dismal
day in a week that had seen rain.' The words, of course, came
from Welsh folk hero and comedian, Max Boyce. His song '9–3'
would be the first track on his first hit album, *Live at Treorchy*,
released in 1974. Max was at the game, no doubt like hundreds
of other 'neutrals', because of the All Blacks. Following the
Llanelli victory, however, he was instrumental in spreading the
impact of that famous win far beyond Sosban territory.

'At that time, I had only just started to sing in clubs in
some areas of south Wales. I had released two albums the
year before, *Max Boyce in Session* and a Welsh-language LP,
Caneuon Amrywiol. But they didn't sell fantastically well.
I had an opportunity, though, to sing on Radio Wales. My
songs at the time weren't so much about rugby as they later
became, and I would sing about different things from day-to-
day life in our communities. In sport, cricket was probably
my biggest passion then and I wrote a song to commemorate
one particular cricketing achievement when I played for Pont-
nedd-fechan in the South Wales League. We were all out for
one run in a game against Skewen! Radio Wales got to hear
about that and that's the first song I sang on the morning

show, *Good Morning Wales*. They said then if I had any other songs on topical issues, to let them know. What I wrote mostly in the early years were industrial ballads, about pit closures especially. I was like a cartoonist in effect, observing what was happening and writing songs about it. That continued after the rugby related songs took off in a big way with *Live at Treorchy* and *We all had Doctors' Papers*, but they didn't seem to get noticed so much!'

Max was working mornings on the match day and finished about an hour early to go to watch the game with some friends. He worked at Metal Box in Neath. The company was founded in England in 1921 and was involved in the production of metal containers. They were soon looking to expand and they headed west, offering hundreds of jobs at a time and in a place where unemployment was high. They bought a tinplate works in Neath and then, when the demand really took off, fuelled by the boom in tinned food, Metal Box built a factory to make the tins next door to the factory that made the tinplate.

After a few years as a coal miner, Max became a Metal Box worker. His workmates remember that this young man with a guitar was soon asked to sing what they called 'little ditties' at Christmas parties. He performed in Welsh rather than English at that time and had many early opportunities to be on Welsh TV programmes. This, in turn, led to invites to go to events in the more Welsh-speaking areas, Llanelli being one of them. As with Ryan and Ronnie, 1971 was the year in which Max raised his profile across both languages, with the release of an English and Welsh album.

'I must have only sung a couple of songs on the radio after that cricket one, but the first big one was the one about the Llanelli game. 'Hymns and Arias' had been recorded in 1971 and was on *Max Boyce in Session*. 'The Devil's Marking Me' was another one. There was an advert for my single, 'Twickers', in the programme of the Llanelli–All Blacks game. But '9–3' was the first song to get any wide attention. That song, if you really look at it, is hardly about the game itself at all. I don't say who scored; I don't mention a charge down try, nothing. It's more about the passion at the game and the effect it had on the town. That's what struck me. I had written most of that song the morning after the game and it was recorded for Radio Wales very soon, probably the Thursday after. I think I've only experienced what I felt like watching that game on two occasions since. There was almost an inevitability that Llanelli were going to win; there was a feeling in the air that the gods were smiling on them that day. I felt exactly the same at the South Africa–New Zealand World Cup final – that famous one which Nelson Mandela attended, and the Welsh Grand Slam when we had to beat Ireland in 2005. Those are the three occasions I've felt something special was happening and a certainty, almost an inevitability, beforehand of what was going to happen.'

One Saturday evening Max was singing in his home club of Glynneath, the team having just played a club from the Llanelli area. After one song, one of the visiting fans stood up and asked Max to sing '9–3'. Max had to admit apologetically that he probably didn't know the words in full any more. This was about 25 years after the game! 'What do you mean, you don't know the words?' The fan was suitably aggrieved, but undeterred. 'I know them all still!' And with that, Max recalls, he proceeded to sing the whole song in front of Max and a full clubhouse. 'When he'd finished, he headed for the door, stopped, turned round and looked at me with a look that obviously meant, what do you mean you can't remember the words? How dare you! I lost a fan that night for certain!'

In case there are a few, like Max, who have now forgotten the words, here they are:

'Twas on a dark and dismal day in a week that had seen rain,
When all roads led to Stradey Park with the All Blacks here again,
They poured down from the valleys, they came from far and wide,
There were 50,000 in the ground and me and Dai outside.

The shops were closed like Sunday and the streets were silent still,
And those who chose to stay away were either dead or ill,
But those who went to Stradey Park will remember 'till they die,
How New Zealand were defeated and how the pubs ran dry.

Oh the beer flowed at Stradey, piped down from Felinfoel,
And the hands that held the glasses high were strong from steel
                                                    and coal,
The air was filled with singing and I heard a grown man cry,
Not because we'd won but because the pubs ran dry.

Then dawned the morning after, on empty factories,
But we were still at Stradey, bloodshot absentees,
But we all had doctors' papers and they all said just the same,
That we all had Scarlet fever and we caught it at the game.

Now all the little babies in Llanelli from now on,
Will be christened Roy or Carwyn, Derek, Delme, Phil or John,
And in a hundred years from now they'll sing a song for me,
About that day the scoreboard read Llanelli 9 Seland Newydd 3.

And when I grow old, my hair turns grey and they put me in a chair,
I'll tell my great-grandchildren that their Dat-cu was there.
And they'll ask to hear the story of that dark October day,
When I went down to Stradey Park and I saw the Scarlets play.

Max's songs and his two hugely influential albums of the
1970s speak about rugby and what it means to be Welsh. He
brings two things together that aren't actually separated in the
day-to-day lives of many. Swansea historian Martin Johnes
has stated that *Live at Treorchy* says as much about Welshness,
in its own right, as does Anglo-Welsh poet Dylan Thomas or
Welsh-language playwright Saunders Lewis. The song '9–3' is
part of that analysis.

The '72 game was to prove influential to another important
part of Welsh rugby heritage. Not only was the game a piece of
the Max Boyce story, but it was also part of the Groggs story
too. Founded in 1969 by the inimitable John Hughes, the world

of clay caricature figures was popular in those early years, but nothing as popular as they are now.

'That All Black tour of 1972/73 and specifically the Llanelli victory against them was pivotal for the Groggs,' explains John's son Richard. 'Up until that time, the characters being done were mainly animals, Celtic characters from the Mabinogion, shepherds, miners, giants in animal skins and the like. They did well, so well that my dad had to move from the garden shed in our house in Trefforest, where he'd started, to new premises. He bought the derelict Dan y Graig pub in Broadway, Pontypridd in 1971. We're still there. By the time Llanelli played the All Blacks we had only done a couple of rugby figures. Some were general ones, such as a front row, but my dad had just started with named players. That was off the back of the Lions tour in 1971 and he made figures of Gareth Edwards and J.P.R. But that was it.'

Richard had caught the rugby bug from his dad and went with him as a 13-year old to watch the seventh All Blacks on a number of occasions. He saw them play Gwent, Glamorgan, Cardiff and Newport. But for some reason, his dad didn't go to the Llanelli game, and Richard went with a friend and a van full of his dad's friends, including one who worked for him.

'My friend and I sat on one of those upturned pop crates with a plank across the top at the Pwll End of the ground. I was separated from the people I went with, but that didn't seem to be a problem at all. I remember thinking what a presence the All Black players were, quite intimidating. The whole game, especially because Llanelli won, made an awesome impression on me as a young boy, and it was quite special to be there. As soon as the whistle blew, I was on the pitch, making a beeline for Delme Thomas. On my way to him, an All Black player trod on my foot – I'll always remember that! I was so excited that after we stopped for chips in Llanelli on the way home, I impatiently threw my brace out of the van window so that I could eat my chips quicker! We had to stop the van then, and go back to search the Llanelli streets for my brace!'

That victory was a significant step in guiding the Groggs company to concentrate on the Welsh rugby characters of the era. John Hughes soon produced a Grogg of victorious captain Delme Thomas in victory salute mode. That is a rare piece today as it's not only the third named-player Grogg from the start of the company, but one done by John himself. Richard was suitably inspired by his dad's work in clay and most definitely enthused by Llanelli's victory that figures were soon to show his work as well as his father's. 'I used to do some figures in the shed at home with dad, as a way of earning some pocket money. But that soon developed to me creating the faces of the characters. Dad would do the body, arms and legs and I would finish off the faces.'

One of the early pieces which Richard was wholly responsible for was of Carwyn James. This is now a very rare piece indeed. 'I did it from photographs after Carwyn died. He's standing up, wearing a Lions tracksuit. The Grogg used to be given out as a man of the match award at Scarlets games for a while. But I have no idea where they are now. Grav asked for one of those Groggs of Carwyn, but he wanted me to put a cigarette in his hand, so that one is even rarer!'

Like Richard Hughes, many who went to see Llanelli play the All Blacks didn't actually support Llanelli. That's what was done then, as the chance of seeing them play didn't come around often and, when it did, it was special. This meant that local rivalries had to be circumnavigated. Welsh historian and sports academic, Peter Stead, went through that process. 'Over the years, I've seen New Zealand play 31 times in all, and lose only 3 times – once to Llanelli, once to England and once to South Africa. That's an astonishing record. I had gone down to Llanelli to see them play by virtue of persuading myself that it was all right to do so as a Swansea fan! Strictly speaking, as a Swansea Jack, I should have been supporting New Zealand, not the Llanelli Turks. But there were some influencing factors. Firstly, many Llanelli players were either from Swansea or had played for the club. Added to that was the fact that Chico

Hopkins came from the same village as my mother, Caerau near Maesteg, and that J.J. Williams came from Nantyffyllon where my auntie lived, made it all right to cross the Loughor bridge. And after my family moved from Gowerton to Pontypridd, I used to watch them play, and they of course had Tommy David in their ranks. So that was another attraction. I felt then that these factors gave me permission to go and see the Scarlets play, it made it legitimate. But secondly, because Carwyn James was at the helm, after masterminding the Lions win in 1971, this game between Llanelli and the All Blacks was elevated to an international level, of international significance, just because of Carwyn's presence. That meant of course that we were all on his side anyway.'

Peter Stead was at Stradey with Stuart Clark, an Englishman, and Jack Spence, a South African. But they too had bought the Llanelli ticket. 'We were at the Pwll End and I'll never forget Stuart balling at the English referee, Mike Titcombe, and calling him all names and me thinking that Stuart was actually English himself! That didn't matter; he was on Llanelli's side! When it got to the second half, we assumed that the All Blacks would fight back and win. But it didn't happen, of course. The lasting image that the three of us have from that game was Phil Bennett sending Grant Batty flying. That day in total, Benny proved that he was a great. We weren't too sure of him before that game, not sure at all if he could fill Barry John's boots. But he convinced us that day.'

Dozens of newspaper column inches around the world heralded Llanelli's success. Broadsheets and red tops alike praised the Llanelli players and their master, Carwyn James. It was good to read those accounts and see the world's rugby press turn their attention to south-west Wales. Anyone who was anyone in any rugby country in the world knew about Llanelli that day. One report, in the Welsh-language weekly magazine, *Y Faner*, was written by a young teacher. Huw Llewelyn Davies would go on to be the voice of rugby for BBC Wales and S4C.

'I was teaching at Llandovery College at the time, having

just had Carwyn James' old job in the Welsh department there. I was also involved with teaching a little rugby as well. There was a warden there at the time, R. Gerallt Jones. He was one of Wales' most prolific Welsh authors in prose and poetry. But he was an ardent sports fan too, cricket mainly, but also rugby. When it was suggested that a group of us should go to see Llanelli play the All Blacks, his was the first name on the bus and the trip was arranged. That's how I succeeded to get to Stradey that day. We took the first team down, along with some members of staff. The fact that Carwyn hadn't long left the school was obviously a big factor as well.'

The group stood together on the Tanner Bank, the best place to be on a day like that according to Huw. By then Huw had started contributing articles to *Y Faner* at the instigation of his father, Eic Davies, a pioneering Welsh-language sports broadcaster. He was responsible for the sports page in the magazine and would encourage his son to contribute now and then. Huw's account of the game is detailed and authoritative. But today, he remembers very little of it. 'I remember the charge down, the try, Andy Hill's penalty and Phil Bennett's 40-yard screw-kick after sidestepping Grant Batty, that's about it. It wasn't much of a game, but the occasion and the significance of the victory were greater than the standard of the game itself.'

Huw's article in *Y Faner* was included in the *Scarlet Fever* publication, a collection of press reports about the victory. Its inclusion was at the insistence of Carwyn James, who wanted a Welsh-language article in the commemorative booklet. By 1974, Huw Llewelyn Davies was working full time for HTV and five years later was with the BBC, where he still works.

Fellow broadcaster Roy Noble was also at that game and he too was a young teacher in those days, yet to embark on an equally successful broadcasting career. He has one clear, if rather oblique memory of that day. 'Obviously I remember the atmosphere, which was incredible especially after the win. But, standing where I was, on the Tanner Bank, one man near us was feeling a bit overcome by such a crowd. In fact, he started to get what could be called a claustrophobia attack of sorts. Enterprising fans nearby somehow found a breeze block somewhere and passed it along to him. He stood on this block, which was enough to lift him above the crowd and give him a sense of space and fresh air to calm his fears! He saw the whole game from that block!'

The game also had a life-changing effect on one person who would go on to become a very popular actress, even though she wasn't at the game herself. The late Margaret John would win the hearts of millions through her performances on BBC Wales' comedy *High Hopes* and then as Doris 'Where's the salad?' in *Gavin and Stacey*. She made these performances in her eighties but she'd had a very successful career for decades before that, appearing in *Z Cars*, *Softly, Softly*, *Coronation Street* and a host of other early TV hits, as well as in the theatre. In 1972, she was in London and she told the story of 31 October to the author over coffee in Swansea's Marriott Hotel.

'I was spending the evening with a friend in London, at her home. Her husband had gone out for the day and we had a lovely time together. Then, quite late into the evening, her husband returned with a friend of his. They both fell into the house, arms round each other, singing at the top of their voices. It was 'Sospan Fach' and whatever else they could remember! The friend of the husband was rejoicing that Llanelli had beaten the All Blacks and turned to me to tell me that fact again. "Oh really" I said, "That's good, what was the score?" He stopped in his tracks, and answered 9–3 but couldn't hide his surprise that I had actually shown an interest and had asked what the score was instead of just saying "oh there's nice" or something similar. I was from Swansea and had enough interest in rugby. Anyway, my question made an impression and we got on really well. We ended up getting married and I have Llanelli beating the All Blacks to thank for that!' Margaret married Ben, who at that time was a member of the orchestra on the Hughie Green programme, *Opportunity Knocks*. It certainly did that night.

But, we cannot pretend that everyone was caught up in the

ecstasy of the victory. In the *Western Mail* newspaper, a letter appeared that tried to throw cold water over everything. The writer, a certain H. Morgan, wanted to complain about what he saw as the inordinate fuss made of Llanelli's win.

He writes, 'I think it exceeds all sense and decency. Press, radio and television have depicted it as a kind of tribal victory over an enemy. Certainly we had the shameful scenes of glee and gloating carried on 'till the next day. Where did sport come in? And where was our chivalrous respect towards a young visiting side, who, far from home, were yet unused to Welsh pitches and the climate? Had these foreigners (for as such they were treated) carefully studied films of Llanelli in action and been primed on every aspect of the Stradey set-up, the result might have been different. There is no doubt about the childish hysteria of the Llanelli supporters. Your paper reports the team's trainer as attributing, in part, the Welsh 1905 win over the New Zealanders, to the Evan Roberts Revival of that time. We know that the Llanelli club favours hymns to God on football occasions, but hardly did we suppose any of its supporters would imagine the Deity intervening on Wales's side at any time in a mere football match, look you. What folly. What xenophobic partisanship.'

H. Morgan came from Swansea.

Summing up the wider impact of that victory at Stradey, the then Wales coach Clive Rowlands does it in a nutshell. He was the very successful coach of Wales in that Seventies golden era. He also was the one responsible for giving the first cap to every one of the Llanelli '72 team who either were, or would be, internationals, apart from Delme Thomas. On the match day, he was in Llanelli early as the Welsh selectors were having a pre-match meal and meeting at the town's Stepney Hotel.

'I went to Llanelli that day as a Welsh selector. But after five minutes of walking through the town after our meeting and lunch, I was a Scarlet supporter. You couldn't help but being so, the town itself was on fire and the enthusiasm was infectious. And then, once inside the ground, the crowd was even more overwhelming. The other thing that made an impression on me was the goat standing with the band at half time! That game was significant, because it didn't only lift the spirits of the Llanelli people, it lifted the spirits of everyone in Wales. It was that big. I left that ground feeling proud that I had at one stage played for Llanelli. But more than that, much more than that, I left feeling proud to be Welsh.'

10

Grav's game

Get your first tackle in early, even if it's late!

Ray Gravell

ON THESE PAGES fourteen players who were on the pitch that day have shared various memories of the momentous victory in '72. But not everyone involved that day are still with us. In 1981, the ever popular physio, Bert Peel, was taken ill during the traditional Boxing Day game against London Welsh at Stradey and passed away later that evening. The coach Carwyn James passed away in tragic circumstances in 1983 at the age of 53. Norman Gale, his assistant, died in 2005. Others involved in various ways on that day have also gone. But one person more than any other, has left a glaring hole in this account of that day, the baby of the team, Ray Gravell. How sad that it was the youngest player that was the first to go.

Many of the players have already recounted Grav related tales from that day and that era. It was obvious that the young centre was already making an impression on his team, especially after settling, that season, into the centre position which he made his own from then on. He played scrum half for Carmarthen Schoolboys, with Roy Bergiers as outside half. He'd taken to the wing at Llanelli for a while. But in September '72, he was in the centre to stay. Under the stand, in the post-match euphoria, sixth former Mark Sayers remembers Grav using the phrase that would be seen on banners in years to come, saying then that he indeed dealt with soft centres.

Team mate Barry Llewelyn tells of the lasting legacy of that game as far as Grav was concerned. 'Grav had his famous pre-match toilet routine, of course, but after that game there was an added dimension to it. He had the squad photo which was taken before playing the All Blacks sellotaped on the back of the toilet door as added inspiration!'

Grav wrote about his experiences in beating the All Blacks in a co-written Welsh-language biography published in 1986, called simply *Grav*. We are, at least, fortunate enough to have his words about that momentous occasion. They were included, in translation, in the volume, *Grav: In his Own Words*, published after his untimely death. The date of his death could not be more ironic or fitting. The youngest man on the pitch on 31 October 1972 died on 31 October 2007.

Grav's funeral was like no other. It was held at Stradey Park and 10,000 people gathered to pay their last respects. It was as close to a state funeral as someone who wasn't a member of a ruling parliament or a Royal family could have. Except, of course, that Grav was Welsh royalty to everyone in Wales.

The then First Minister of Wales, Rhodri Morgan took part, as did rugby elder statesman, Gerald Davies, and former arch-druid, Meirion Evans. His coffin was carried by some Scarlet greats, including the captain in '72, Delme Thomas, and two others who played that day, Derek Quinnell and Gareth Jenkins. Before his illness, Grav had been the keeper of the sword during the National Eisteddfod's official ceremonies. The sword is always kept in its sheath to signify peace. That duty was handed over to Robin McBryde when Grav was unable to continue. At the funeral Robin stood holding the sword out in front of him, unflinchingly, for the whole service. It was quite an imposing sight. This was the only time the sword had been allowed to be used outside the Eisteddfod; special permission was granted so that the sword could be part of the service to mark Grav's passing. Grav's coffin was followed into the ground by his wife Mari and his daughters,

Manon and Gwenan, both wearing Scarlet jerseys with Grav's number on the back. It was an extremely emotional day.

On that day, in November 2007, the scoreboard showed the famous Llanelli 9 Seland Newydd 3 score. Less than a year later, in October 2008, the last game was played at Stradey and the club moved to new pastures. Grav was involved with negotiating that move as the then president of the club. But he would not see the new beginnings. He was to go hand-in-hand with the old. The score of the '72 game was the final testament on that famous scoreboard the very last time Grav left the sacred Stradey turf.

Grav's memories of the game are told with his usual enthusiasm and honesty. Some facts differ from those of his team mates. But they aren't crucial ones. There's no surprise that his first comments were ones of self-doubt and questioning. They were evidently there right from the start: he thinks that he might not have been good enough to be chosen to play against the All Blacks. Llanelli were into the 1972/73 season with three wings in effect (which would not be enough these days), but then it was a cause for concern if you were number three and especially if you had Grav's insecurities. Andy Hill was well established, J.J. had been brought in and Grav was at that time a winger. The centre positions were usually filled by Bernard Thomas and Roy Bergiers. Ray was worried about his role in all this. 'I started worrying again about my place in the team. Was I a centre after all? Although Carwyn had said many times that a strong wing was necessary to face Bryan Williams of New Zealand, I was very reluctant to consider myself in that position... In any case, during the last weeks of September, Bernard Thomas injured his knee and, after a while, the selectors were obliged to pick me as Roy's partner at centre.'

Grav would often joke that when the fit again Bernard Thomas was occasionally chosen instead of him at centre, Carwyn had only done so because Bernard was better-looking than him – telling words.

So, Grav was the first-choice centre for that All Blacks game and in that game, as in many others to follow, he did eat soft centres. He remembers the day the team was announced and remembers a fact that none of the other players have mentioned to date. 'The week before the match, with Carwyn now lecturing at Trinity College, Carmarthen, the selectors – Carwyn, Norman, Delme and the chairman Handel Greville – met for lunch at the Ivy Bush Hotel in Carmarthen and announced the Scarlets team.'

The fact it was a week earlier, that he refers to Handel Greville as a selector, and that he also mentions where the team was announced, differs from all other accounts. Handel Greville would probably have been there, but he was not a selector – that is certain. The reference that it happened a week earlier might well be true, as most of the other players couldn't remember very well. Those that did remember thought it was on the Sunday before the game, as noted earlier. In Grav's favour is the fact that he wrote these words only 14 years after the events happened.

But, TV footage from a documentary HTV filmed about Carwyn, which included filming on 31 October, shows Carwyn addressing the team and saying that he, Delme and Norman had met the night before to choose the team. Therefore, the announcement of the team on the Sunday before the game could not be true as they were returning from Gloucester then. So, Grav is probably right with regards the timing of the announcement. But he is not correct about the location. The footage shows them clearly to be in a room at Stradey. It's definitely not the Ivy Bush!

On the Saturday before the game some players didn't make the trip to Gloucester, through injury or other commitments. But Grav was there and the visit had a huge impact on him, referring to it as 'another sign of Carwyn's meticulous coaching... Although his personal organisational skills were poor, Carwyn insisted on perfect arrangements for his players at all times – lunch would be prepared for us in a hotel before we went to watch the match. I had the chance to watch the giants from the far ends of the earth for the first time since my father took me to Stradey in 1963. Then, through a child's eye, the players seemed enormous, but at Gloucester that Saturday afternoon – although they won the match easily and displayed remarkable skills – I realised that they were mere mortals and that it was possible to beat them.'

Grav enthuses about the conversation on the bus on the way home and, as the other players have done, points to a very positive mood in their midst on the long journey from Gloucester to Llanelli. They all agreed that they hadn't seen anything that could intimidate them or make them think that they weren't up to the job in hand. He does, however, add his own contribution. 'Looking back from the present, I would be prepared to say that planning the trip that afternoon to the west of England was the greatest psychological aid that he gave us in all the preparations.'

Great words indeed. Any psychological aid, however, was easily undermined in Grav's case by his psychological insecurities. One thing that certainly unnerved him was the build-up to the Llanelli game in the press. He says how it affected him personally, 'I must admit that the press coverage affected me too, because when the *Western Mail* published photographs of the visitors, I began studying my opponents' height and weight. Usually, if my opponents were quite big, I'd start worrying. But with time, I realised that I shouldn't believe every word I read in the papers – a few players turned out to be much smaller than expected on the field!'

But if he wasn't overawed by the size of the opponents as much as he feared, he was bowled over by the events immediately before the kick-off. He recalls vividly the team get-together at the Ashburnham Hotel and the speeches by club president Handel Greville, Ray Williams from the WRU, and Carwyn himself. He makes one very interesting observation about the captain's famous speech. The players spoken to for this book were fairly divided as to where that speech took

place. The consensus seems to be at the Ashburnham itself.
But, here's how Grav recalls things happened at the hotel.
'Delme wasn't given a chance to speak – and I'm sure in my
mind that Carwyn did this on purpose. He wanted to keep
Delme's words back until the last minute in the changing room,
as Delme was the only one allowed to speak there.'

That sounds fairly conclusive, but flies in the face of Delme
Thomas' own version of events! The captain recalls talking at
the Ashburnham Hotel. Some players share Grav's account of
events, others share Delme's. It turns out that Delme spoke on
both occasions. What is beyond question, of course, is what
Delme said and the impact those words had on the 15 men
who took to the field.

After a tactical team talk by Carwyn in the hotel, the journey
on the bus from Burry Port to Stradey was next. All the players
speak of the overwhelming sight of fans lining the road, and
thronging to the match on foot from miles around and hours
in advance. This certainly bowled Grav over. 'I got on the bus
and sat in the front seat; my mind drifted off and butterflies
began fluttering in my stomach. When Delme got on, he sat
next to me – the captain had obviously seen fear or panic or
something else in my face. The next minute, he put a fatherly
arm around my shoulder and said, "Don't worry about bugger
all Grav bach – everything will be OK, boy."'

Grav always had a special affection for Delme and Delme
looked after him in this fatherly way whenever possible. Grav
always used to insist on following Delme onto the pitch, when
he led them out as captain. Andy Hill would always insist on
being third out, behind Delme and Ray. Quite often, the other
players would let Ray walk down the tunnel behind Delme,
only to pull him back by the shirt and stop him in order to
wind him up – which it always did, of course. But they didn't
try any such tricks as they walked onto the pitch to play the All
Blacks.

Once on the pitch, new fears kicked in, new even for Grav.
There might well have been about 25,000 people there robed in

scarlet and white, but Grav was totally transfixed by the sea of black one side of the pitch. 'I saw nothing but a sea of faces and black shirts and felt a wall of sound as we reached our theatre that afternoon. It was the coliseum brought to life in 20th-century Wales. During those few seconds, I was overwhelmed by a sense of fear, which completely surrounded me and the only thing going through my mind was "How can I get out of here?" For a short while, and for the only time in my life, I had an attack of claustrophobia.'

It was the referee's whistle which shook him out of his reverie, and the game was on. Grav's account of the game itself is similar enough to the other players, as is the account of the aftermath. His language, however, is different to all the others. He's already referred to 'the afternoon's theatre'. In summing up the victory he says, 'If James released Excalibur from the stone in New Zealand in 1971, he crushed the stone to bits this time.' He would also refer to the game as having '... all the ingredients for a classic fairy tale...' or '... a 20th-century re-enactment of David and Goliath...'. These, indeed, were the kind of words that would not be alien to the thinking man himself, Carwyn James. Grav was evidently under his influence in more ways than one.

Even in 1986, before the amateur era was over, Grav was ready to admit that he was given a substantial amount of money for that game. Having already referred to the occasion as the first time he had ever worn a kit that was specially prepared for the club, he later said, 'I was given an envelope, with the largest sum of money I had ever received from the club – ten pounds of beer money. It was the first time I had held a ten-pound note.'

Most of the match day photos in this book were taken by Alan T. Richards and we've heard his match day story. Many, many photographers took that squad photo before the game. But the pre-match team photo included in this book is an unmistakeable Alan Richards original. Why? Because of Grav.

All the other squad members and coaches are looking

towards the bank of photographers from newspapers far and wide. Grav is looking straight down the lens of Alan's camera and, therefore, in a different direction to everyone else. Alan had become good friends with Ray while running the touchline to take his photographs. On that momentous day, Grav wanted to look out for his friend, the local man who was there every game, come rain or shine. So while all his team mates look in the same direction, Grav looks at Alan. Thirty-five years later, Alan remembers exactly where he was when he heard of Grav's death. 'I was in Gorseinon; my wife Margaret and I had gone to the shops. I had stopped the car and my wife had started her way to the chemist to get a prescription while I turned the engine off and locked up. As I turned the engine off, the radio was still on and I couldn't believe what I heard. I was totally numb. It said that Ray Gravell was dead. When I saw my wife, she could see that I was shaken. I shared the news and we both felt the grief. Still in a state of shock, we had one more call to make in the supermarket before going home. Our grandson was with us as well, and I walked round some aisles as my wife walked round some others. My grandson was with me as I tried to step over a pallet that was on the floor in front of me. Out of the blue, with no warning, I felt a terrible pain and I collapsed, unable to move. I told my grandson to go and get my wife as I clung on to a freezer next to me.'

An ambulance was called and Alan was taken to hospital. He had suffered a stroke, less than an hour after learning of his friend Grav's death. As a result he was not well enough to go to Grav's funeral. The medical staff at the hospital offered to take him, in his bed, down to the TV lounge to see Grav's funeral on television. He didn't feel up to that at all and listened to it on the radio instead. Back home, his wife recorded the funeral for him from the television, so that he could watch it once he was out of hospital. Five years later, Alan has still not been able to bring himself to watch that video.

At Grav's funeral, alongside the dignitaries already mentioned, one touching contribution was made by Welsh singer-songwriter, Gwyneth Glyn. She sung one of her own songs called 'Adra' (Home). With a haunting purity that resonated around Stradey in a most moving way, she sang about different versions of home mentioned in popular songs. The refrain said that 'There was nowhere quite like home they say, But home is very much like you.' As she sang images of Grav's coffin, Robin McBryde bearing the Eisteddfod sword, Ray's hero – folk singer Dafydd Iwan, his wife and children and that famous 9–3 scoreboard moved through the minds of the tens of thousands marking his passing. Grav. Stradey. Home.

11

The thinking
man's game

There is no gainsaying the romantic view as to who is the most
admired coach in rugby – Carwyn James of Wales.

Mick Cleary, *Daily Telegraph*, 2007

HAVING TRAVELLED FROM England with the New Zealand
team, journalist Terry McLean spent his first day in Wales
at the home of Carwyn James. The two were like-minded.
Reading Terry McLean's stories of the '72 tour, his style, and
his references to poetry, theatre and music suggests that he
and Carwyn both enjoyed and understood rugby, and lived
similar lives. He was the *New Zealand Herald*'s man on the tour,
and it was the twenty-third All Black tour he had covered in
twenty-two years. In 1973, he published a book about the '72
tour, the title of which sums up his attitude to the way the
All Blacks conducted themselves – *They Missed the Bus*. In a
chapter headed 'March of the Little Saucepan', he speaks of
that time he spent at Carwyn's home, on the Sunday before
Llanelli played the All Blacks, in this way, 'I spent the night in
talks with Carwyn, his older sister, Gwen, and their mother,
an elderly lady in her seventies who is so very Welsh that to
this day she prefers the Welsh rather than the English for her
conversation.'

It's a very homely picture, which says so much about

Carwyn himself and the community from which he came – the same community which gave the world that other All Blacks conqueror, Barry John. Terry McLean also spent time having tea with Barry John's parents that day and visited Cefneithin Rugby Club. On the Monday, he met Carwyn for lunch in Carmarthen, along with a few of Carwyn's friends, and he describes his time in Wales' oldest market town as a 'dip into another world of strangely rural sweetness'. During his two days in that Welsh-speaking rural family-orientated community, Terry got to understand a little of the culture which had given the world such a rugby legacy and so many rugby legends.

'The one thing which remained salient in my mind was the talk by Gwen and Carwyn of how they remembered, as children, seeing their father come home daily from the pit, black from the coal he had worked in, and changing, with scrubbing, into near normality; they remembered too the first signs of the silicosis which was to eat through his lungs and his life, lingeringly, painfully, so that when Gwen, two or three years before he died, quitted her London work as a psychiatric nurse so that she might attend upon her father, there had to be oxygen to help him through the bad times. They had the talk, too, of the average Welshman of Carwyn's and earlier generations, the man who entered the pits as a boy not older that fourteen and who, by the time he was thirty-five, was already in the throes of phthisis, the dreaded killer of the pits.'

For us today, with the pits long gone from our landscapes and from the psyche of the younger generations, these words might sound a little sentimental. But they were written forty years ago by a man who could understand what he saw and heard. There's no doubting the impression left on Terry McLean by his time in Carmarthenshire. He continues, 'Who could doubt that a people living in intangible but constant fear that a beam might give, a rock face fall or, perhaps worst of all, dust creep into lungs, would acquire some special qualities of determination and resolution.' Whatever the external joviality or warmth, he says, underneath is steel and he then asks in conclusion, 'How could the true Welsh be anything else?'

This is how he understood Carwyn James – the man who had masterminded four defeats of New Zealand in three years: two Tests, the victory with his club Llanelli and with the Barbarians, not forgetting the one drawn Test in New Zealand in 1971 too. So in six games he'd only lost once. No one else had such a record.

At the end of the 1971 tour, Carwyn James was rightly venerated by the rugby world. The New Zealanders, hurting as they were, could still recognise the greatness of Carwyn James. New Zealand's *The Dominion and Sunday Times* publication, 'Britain's Finest Lions' praises the maestro's achievements at every opportunity. One piece is entitled, 'Carwyn James: Thank You'. They sum up his contribution, 'He has that great attribute (charisma if you like) of having men who want to please him. This he does not trade on but rather gives back knowledge-in-detail ways of putting it into effect and confidence born of ability. Thank you Carwyn James – you have won our hearts in spite of beating our players.'

A few references are made in 'Britain's Finest Lions' to a debate which was obviously going on in Britain at the time about rugby coaches. One journalist says, 'If there is now a reluctance to adopt coaching in Britain, this man surely is the best argument against it.' Added to Carwyn's previous comments about selection, the squad system and the fixture list, it becomes apparent that there was a debate about what a coach's function was amongst rugby clubs at the time. Then Wales coach Clive Rowlands also came into the debate. He coached the national side for 29 matches from 1968 to 1974, which included the Grand Slam in 1971.

'I captained Wales for three years and, as captain, in those days you were the coach as well. I had to run the sessions completely myself. I was a PE teacher anyway, so that was part of my qualification for the role, as happened then. When I was appointed coach officially, the first thing I did was to call those responsible for the Welsh clubs together to discuss how they thought the game should go. Carwyn was one of them.'

Clive Rowlands was only the second official Wales coach, Dai Nash being the first. So when the Welsh embarked on their Seventies golden era, it was with only the second man to be called Wales coach in the game's near hundred-year history. Carwyn's role with the Lions had influenced, if not Clive Rowlands' selection, the broader debate about the role of a coach. Lions '71 captain, John Dawes, sums it up in this way. 'The word "coach" was not in the rugby vocabulary. There were coaches in New Zealand and South Africa but these countries were regarded as "too professional". (England's equivalent was Don Rutherford – labelled technical administrator.) The 1971 tour changed attitudes in UK rugby, especially towards coaching. Coaching now became acceptable and the way forward. In Wales, Clive Rowlands was at the helm and enjoying success with the Welsh team. At the end of his first three-year period as coach, Clive was given the option of another three years and quite naturally and deservedly he took it. Carwyn had reportedly stated that he wanted to choose the team without the help of the Big Five. Whether or not that is factual remains uncertain, but it did seem logical that when Clive stood down Carwyn should become national coach.'

Throughout the Seventies, Wales coach Clive Rowlands took a fair degree of criticism for his perceived role in keeping Carwyn from the Wales job. Looking back at that period, it's obvious that that grieved Clive Rowlands, who was no different to anyone else within the game in his admiration for Carwyn. 'People used to come up to me and tell me that it was terrible what I was doing to Carwyn. It wasn't very pleasant, I can tell you. What did people expect me to do, make Wales deliberately start to lose so that he could be chosen? It's the clubs, large and small, who, for their own political reasons didn't vote Carwyn onto the WRU. They are the ones accountable.'

Things were changing within the game and the success of the Lions, with Carwyn as the mastermind, moved the game on

raph, five years ago, Mick Cleary
es. 'Never mind all that romantic
...ity, his intellect, his mystic Welshness.
...had been no more than a wistful dreamer,
...ll be talking about him now. He was the coach
...uded the Lions to victory in New Zealand, the Stradey
Park sage who gave Llanelli its most famous day. He was an
achiever, a pragmatist as well, a man who got the best out of
people, a coach who inspired players to reach out beyond their
own limitations, surely the essence of what constitutes a good
coach. Sadly, those small men running Welsh rugby never felt
the same way about Carwyn. He was a prophet without honour
in Wales, destined never to coach the national team.'

The Rugby Royalty website comments, 'Anyone who
may think that the rugby coach did little back in the days of
amateurism, may be true to an extent, but in the case of James,
he was definitely a hands-on man and one of the visionaries
of rugby and helped to shape a lot of the good things in rugby
that still exist today.'

In Llanelli, there was one other early sign of things to come.
Les Williams was watching Llanelli play, making notes of the
scorers and the score when Carwyn spotted him. 'Carwyn
came up to me one day, obviously having watched me do this
and asked what I was doing. I told him and he asked me if I
would make more detailed notes about line-outs and scrums,
as well as the score. I did, of course, and then handed the
notes to Carwyn at the end of every game. That was very early,
primitive analysis which is done today by professionals with
modern technology. But Carwyn started that at Llanelli in the
early 1970s, with me scribbling on a pad!'

In today's coaching terms, however, the '72 game looks
nothing like being a part of a pioneering process. When Nigel
Davies was head coach at the Scarlets, he sat with club analyst,
Gareth Potter, and watched a recording of the '72 game;
they analysed it as they would analyse any game in today's
professional era. The findings were astounding. The ball was

live on the field of play for less than ten minutes. Phase play was unknown then anyway, and there are no instances of the ball going beyond the second phase at all.

The second youngest player who faced the All Blacks, Gareth Jenkins, would go on to coach Llanelli himself and was at the helm in one of the club's most successful seasons ever. There is another anniversary this year for the club – it's twenty years since they beat the then world champions, Australia. Gareth Jenkins was the coach that day. 'It's obvious that I did pick up so much from Carwyn – you couldn't help but doing so. I had developed as a player with Carwyn coaching us in his way, so that was the way I knew. I particularly bought into the attitude of mind that it was crucial to always be thinking and to think in terms of the bigger picture. It was essential to have an outlook. The way that he built up the preparation for that one game against the All Blacks over a period of months, if not years, is the best example of that you could have.'

Carwyn would call to see Gareth at his home during the week, and the conversation showed Carwyn had one clear focus. 'He was talking in those early days about leadership potential for me. He would encourage me, nurture me and help me develop as an individual with that end in mind. He'd talk rugby philosophy with me as a 20-year-old! How valuable was that!'

Carwyn's ability to deal appropriately with an individual is something that the players, without exception, have noted. He knew when a gentle word was needed, or a sterner one – when encouragement or motivation was the best tool. 'Carwyn would make us think for ourselves,' says Delme Thomas, 'and ask us why we did such and such a thing, make us come up with answers of our own so that we, through that, would not only have the answer, but the understanding as well. That's what you needed out on the pitch when the coach was in the stand.'

Many of the players referred to another attribute, the ability to deal with emotions. They testify to his way of letting them feel emotion before a game – the All Blacks game is an excellent case in point – but not to let that emotion rule once they were on the pitch. But neither did he want them to leave it in the dressing room. He taught us, as one said, 'to deal with our emotions on the pitch as well'.

But, to return to Terry McLean and his view of Carwyn's world: Carwyn's record as a technical coach is beyond question; his man management of players way ahead of its time. However, by spending time with Carwyn at his home village, Terry McLean saw more than the rugby brain. He saw that family and community were central to Carwyn and he also saw tensions and pressures that didn't come from rugby. A few years ago, S4C produced a drama-documentary about Carwyn's life and concluded, 'Despite all his success in life, Carwyn is shown to be a troubled individual with emotional tensions, a complicated and lonely man whose success in the macho world of rugby masked unendurable physical and emotional torment.'

Looking back over 40 years, some of Carwyn's squad at Llanelli can see early signs of some of those needs. Phil Bennett, in particular, remembers a specific pattern in Carwyn's life. 'Quite regularly, there would be a knock on the door of our home in Felinfoel, around nine o'clock in the evening. It was Carwyn, sometimes with a bottle of wine in his hand, other times we would just have a cup of coffee. He'd come in, make himself comfortable and Pat would make him a sandwich and we would sit there and we'd chat for hours about all sorts, but mainly rugby, of course. Often, he would fall asleep in the chair, wake up flustered and make his way home, sometimes well after midnight. You couldn't help getting the impression that there was a loneliness there, aching inside him. It was that time of night when he should be thinking of heading home. But it was as if he couldn't. We were fulfilling a role for him.'

Other players note Carwyn visiting for chats and he stays over with some too. Roy 'Shanto' Thomas says that Carwyn would stay with his family if on a speaking engagement somewhere in the Gower area. This dependency is something that resonates with Carwyn's successor at Llandovery College, Huw Llewelyn Davies. 'Immediately after my interview for the job with warden R. Gerallt Jones, Carwyn happened to be visiting Llandovery. He'd been coming back for about a year after starting at Trinity, in order to take some Welsh classes in the evenings. He came up to me on learning that I'd got the job, and said "Congratulations, you'll have a fantastic time here." He then added, with some significance, "But don't make the same mistake as me, don't stay here too long or you will never be able to leave." Over the years, the meaning of those words became evident. He'd obviously found it difficult to let go. He had a broad family there, a community that evidently gave him security. He was a housemaster and was well respected. Llandovery literally was in a world of its own and Carwyn felt safe there.'

He maintained a certain degree of that sense of safety at Trinity College, as he did at the club environment in Llanelli. There, within the macho world of rugby, he instilled what could be called family values in his own quiet way. Not only would he benefit from end of the day visits to players' homes, but the players would benefit from his caring attitude as well. Phil and Pat Bennett were newly married at that time, and were in their first home together. 'A while after we got married, we had the tragedy of losing a little one. We were obviously devastated. Carwyn was so sympathetic not just towards me, but Pat also. He'd be more patient with me in training and in matches. He could see that I wasn't doing too well in coping with the whole thing, neither of us were. Then, one day, there was that knock on the door again and it was Carwyn. He came in, sat down, and asked us how we were and then asked, surprisingly, what we were doing in a few weeks' time. We looked puzzled at him and said nothing was planned, obviously. At which point he handed us an envelope which included a ticket for the two of us to go abroad for a week. He said that we needed to get away from everything and have time to recover. That was a completely overwhelming gesture. We went and it was the best thing that we could have done, thanks to Carwyn's foresight.'

That same attitude was shown towards Chico Hopkins at another time of personal tragedy. 'I had joined Llanelli and there were only a few weeks to go to the All Blacks game. We were playing in Cross Keys. Half time arrived and I could see Carwyn walking over to us players on the pitch. That was rather unusual and then he asked me to go off the field. I didn't think I had played that badly! Anyway, subs weren't allowed then, except for injury, and I knew I wasn't injured. He could see I didn't quite get what was going on and he said that my father had been taken ill. I had gone to the game in the car with my father and brother from Maesteg. I followed Carwyn, and when we got to the touchline, Carwyn had to break the news to me that my father had actually passed away. He just fell down dead, watching the game, standing next to my 14-year-old brother. You can imagine the effect that had on me and him. Going home from Cross Keys, without our father to tell our mother what had happened, was awful.'

That tragedy hit the Hopkins family hard. Chico has no doubt that it affected his play for Llanelli after that. 'I had tremendous support from Carwyn, he was very patient and understanding. Personally, I didn't think that I would be up to playing the All Blacks at all, because my head was all over the place. But Carwyn used what had happened as a motivation instead of an obstacle. He persevered with me and I obviously did play and had a fairly good game.'

A few weeks after the October victory, Chico was to leave Llanelli and go north to play rugby league, joining Swinton for £8,000. In his mind, that move was a direct link to the passing of his father. 'My father would always encourage me throughout my career. I had an offer to go north the previous season and my dad was all for it. When the offer came after he died, I grabbed it with both hands, thinking I was doing something that my father wanted and would be proud of. I probably wouldn't have gone otherwise and would have stayed with Llanelli. That's probably what I should have done.'

Years later, Chico was to suffer a nervous breakdown, which he put down as a reaction to the tragedy that shook his family in '72. He says that things would have been a lot worse if Carwyn hadn't shown his support during the eye of the storm.

Each player from the '72 team says that Carwyn did one specific thing to change the culture of the club in Llanelli: he involved the wives and girlfriends at every opportunity in club events. 'What he started doing,' explains Angela Davies, Roger's wife, 'was to arrange for us to go a couple of times each season to games against Coventry or Northampton. We would go up with the supporters on the Saturday morning and then join the boys for a meal after the game. We'd come back with them on the Sunday. We also went away when the boys used to go to Saundersfoot training or occasions like that.'

'There was one occasion, in the 1972/73 season, that as players we all went to Llandovery College to train,' recalls Roger Davies. 'This was in preparation for the Cup final at the end of the season, the first of many wins for us. Then, after we'd finished, Carwyn said that we were off to Glansevin. This was a mansion house between Llangadog and Llandovery which used to put on traditional Welsh evenings. He'd also arranged for all the wives and girlfriends to be there as well.'

'As wives or girlfriends, we had been there before the boys, and had afternoon tea there,' explains Angela. 'Then they arrived and we had the full Welsh evening that the place was known for, which involved traditional Welsh food, folk dancing, singing – it was a great night.'

'When the boys got there, we felt that we needed to ask Carwyn if it was all right for us to drink,' adds Roger. 'After a few beers, someone asked if we could have a bottle of wine and Carwyn said OK. We didn't stay that late, but it was a really good evening and certainly different for a rugby team to do. Anyway, when the club had the bill, Carwyn was asked apparently to explain the bottles of wine specifically, but only because the bill was so high! His answer was, "I'll speak to you after next Saturday" which was the day of the Cup final. Of course, we won and nothing more was heard about the Glansevin bill!'

At the end of that season, the wives and girlfriends were taken on the club's trip to Canada. That was an extremely unusual step for a club to take. 'We had only just got married, a few days before,' Angela says, 'and Hefin Jenkins and his wife had just got married a few days before us. So going to Canada with Llanelli Rugby Club was the honeymoon for two couples! There were a couple of occasions when Carwyn had to remind the boys that they were there to play rugby!'

Marlston Morgan played his part in family relations as well on that tour. 'When we got to the hotel, my wife and I had a lovely room with a double bed. But Hefin and his wife had a room with two single beds. So, seeing that they were newly married, my wife and I thought it only right to offer to swap rooms! Needless to say, they didn't refuse!'

Delme Thomas sums up Carwyn's thinking behind such unusual moves, saying that Carwyn was of the opinion that if the home was happy for husband and wife, then the player would play better. Involving the partners was seen as central to team harmony.

British and Irish Lion, John Dawes, has this to say about this aspect of Carwyn's personality. 'Rugby was never a job for Carwyn, it was his life and he wanted people to share that life. Carwyn was a sensitive, educated soul, but through it all his greatness and humanity shone brightly.'

The irony in Carwyn's own personal life, however, is that he gave up that kind of support which he showed to others. He left Llandovery. He would leave Llanelli. He would leave that community described by Terry McLean. That 'safety' that Huw Llywelyn Davies spoke of was gone. There was no safety net anymore. Once in Cardiff, in a flat on his own, starting a broadcasting and journalistic career, he soon turned to that place where lonely people drink together.

He also had issues relating to his own sexuality to deal with. They were never openly discussed but his sister, a former psychiatric nurse, could see that there were things troubling her brother and she had a good idea what they were. Others in the family would deny any suggestion that he was gay, and still do. He also had something else to deal with, something new not just to him but to rugby in general: adulation, following success on the field of play. The attention that the Lions received on their arrival back in Britain had not been seen in the game before.

'On returning to the UK,' says John Dawes, 'the welcome received by the 1971 Lions at Heathrow was immense and totally unexpected. Press and media coverage of the tour, as far as the Lions were concerned, was somewhat limited and this touring team was expected to join the ranks of other tours as 'good tourists' but as Test series losers. To return as series winners was outstanding – but that was never fully appreciated by the players until Heathrow was reached.'

Carwyn would have been personally greeted by the whole village of Cefneithin on his return home, with a carnival atmosphere and a pony and trap to carry him through the streets. Huw Llewelyn Davies lived opposite Gareth Edwards in Gwauncaegurwen, and testifies to the same welcome home for their own Lion.

A young Max Boyce remembers another rare event, evidence of the public clamour to see their Lions heroes. 'I was pretty much unknown really, in 1971, but the Lions manager, Doug Smith, had asked Carwyn to go on a speaking tour of rugby clubs in the south-east of England. I was then invited to go along; I think Carwyn had seen me on Welsh TV or something, and we went up in Carwyn's Renault 12! We did about six nights in different rugby clubs – Carwyn being the raconteur on all sorts of topics and me singing my songs – to an English audience. That was great for me personally and, looking back, of course, a very special opportunity to share such an event with the great man himself.'

Imagine then, the escalation of the adulation for Carwyn when his club side also beat New Zealand. It must have been, literally, unbearable at times. Not only was it new, with the full impact that that would have had, but it also went against Carwyn's very nature. He was not shy of public attention and could command a public speaking platform to any size of audience: he stood as a Plaid Cymru candidate for Llanelli in 1970 and he would later broadcast. But through all of this he was not an extrovert. And, being in the full glare of the public's headlights, while you have issues going on inside your own head and the safe place is far away, can be a complex and cruel place to be.

When Carwyn died in tragic circumstances, alone in a hotel room in Amsterdam, Wales lost a giant. Tributes galore were paid then and have been over the years since. Max Boyce was asked by Carwyn's family to write something for a memorial event that was to be held in Cefneithin Rugby Club. At first, Max turned the offer down, as he didn't feel he could bring himself to write anything at such a time. But, inspiration came at the last minute, drawn from the fact that Max very much regretted not having seen Carwyn for a while before he died. The first and last verses are as follows:

His outspoken views weren't welcome by all
Though the ones who disliked him were few
He could have picked the Welsh team all from Llanelli
And disbanded the WRU! ...

And I wished I'd have seen him a few days before,
Roedd Carwyn yn bartner, yn ffrind –
Just to share one last story, and say, 'James,
Gin bach, cyn i ti fynd.'

12

Why this game?

The whole point of rugby is that it is,
first and foremost, a state of mind, a spirit.

Jean-Pierre Rives, legendary French flanker turned sculptor

AND SO WE return to the question raised in the first chapter. Why has this game seemingly achieved such a status over and above similar games at other clubs? Max Boyce puts it this way, 'I'm intrigued as to why the legend hasn't attached itself to other club victories against New Zealand in the same way as it has to Llanelli's win. Why would that be, I wonder? The players themselves meet for occasional reunions without a doubt, but the broader impact doesn't seem to have been the same for those other victories over the years.'

Max asks the question which has been on so many minds over forty years. But he is actually a part of the answer as well, on two levels. Firstly, he helped the process of spreading the word about '9–3' to an audience far wider than those who wore scarlet. By having a song on Radio Wales two days after the win, he kept the momentum going across Wales. But also, more unwittingly even to Max himself, his songs fitted into a broader pattern in the Celtic countries specifically, as he himself has become aware of over the years.

'The three Celtic rugby nations, Wales, Ireland and Scotland have adopted songs as their own unofficial anthems, or their second anthem if you like. 'Flower of Scotland', 'The Fields of Athenry' and 'Hymns and Arias' have become their anthems at rugby grounds. What's interesting about all three songs is that they were written in the same period and that they came from folk singers in each individual country. 'Flower of Scotland' was written by Roy Williamson, a Scottish songwriter and folk musician. He'd also played rugby for Edinburgh Wanderers and later was a member of the folk group, The Corries. 'Flower of Scotland' was first sung in Scotland's name when Scottish international winger, Billy Steele, asked his team mates to sing it on the Lions tour of South Africa in 1974. 'The Fields of Athenry' was written in the 1970s by Pete St John, an Irish folk singer-songwriter. His real name was Pete Mooney. And in Wales, I wrote 'Hymns and Arias'. It was recorded in 1971, but didn't catch on 'till later. The song '9–3' was a stepping-stone on the road to 'Hymns and Arias' taking off. There seemed to be a desire at the time for the three countries to find their own voice, literally, and since that decade all three countries have a song of their own to say who they are at rugby games.'

An integral part of any folk tradition is the potency of its myths. There are plenty such stories linked with both Llanelli as a club and the game in '72. We've mentioned the myths surrounding the birth of 'Sosban Fach' song. Then there's the myth of the centenary year. The match itself threw up some more – where did Delme give his famous speech? When was the team announced? And when did they actually go to Glansevin, wives and all? There's one more, hitherto unmentioned one. Many players recall facing up to the infamous haka at Stradey. But the All Blacks didn't perform it before that game. According to Fox, Bogle and Hoskins and Terry McLean, the only time the All Blacks did the haka on that tour was before the Barbarians game, right at the end of their stay. Myths are an important part of any legend and that game was not short of a myth or two.

But, before a ball was kicked in anger in October '72, the seeds of the answer to 'why that game' had already been sown. On the back of the Lions victory in '71, all eyes were always going to be on Stradey that day, way before any result was known. Why? Because the mastermind of the All Blacks' downfall in '71 was now trying to do the same with his club team, Llanelli. Expectations from Carwyn were high. People wanted to see how the same man would fare with a club team – the same as he had with the best that Britain and Ireland could offer? No doubt some were expecting him to fail, or at least they didn't have any hope that he would succeed. Carwyn is, of course, the one single answer given when asked about the significance of the '72 victory. But we've already seen that he was brought into a club that was already innovative and pioneering. As immeasurable and as unique his contribution was, and without minimising it in any way, the Carwyn factor wasn't the only factor.

For one thing, coinciding with this expectation was a technological development which heightened the anticipation. Rugby on television was new. The game would have made a poor spectacle on the small screen throughout the Sixties; rugby was only occasionally broadcast live, such as Newport's defeat of the All Blacks in 1963.

But things were changing. Again, the Lions in '71 had captured the country's imagination. Although not broadcast live, the games were watched avidly when they were shown – the obvious success of the team making for more pleasant, enthusiastic viewing. Historian John Davies, in *Broadcasting and the BBC in Wales*, says that by the early 1970s, rugby was starting to become the cornerstone of BBC Wales' coverage, adding that, 'Wales was fortunate in its rugby commentators. David Parry-Jones was considered to be superb, and there was annoyance in Cardiff when London preferred to employ the less talented Nigel Starmer Smith.'

Luckily, David Parry-Jones was asked to commentate on the Llanelli–All Backs game. John Davies goes on to say that Welsh-language commentary also caught on early, thus establishing a foothold in both languages. He adds, 'Welsh broadcasters considered the rugby authorities to be far more co-operative than those of association football, although soccer devotees believed that the BBC in Wales to be excessively biased in favour of rugby. There was some truth in the accusation, for during Welsh rugby's great years BBC Wales saw it as an instrument of nation building.' Rugby broadcasting, by the early 1970s, was seen as significant as rugby itself had been a century earlier. The expectation ahead of the Llanelli–All Blacks game was felt in New Zealand as well. They paid £7,500 to take a live feed of the game from Llanelli, a significant sum of money in those days. In summing up how the Lions victory heaped attention on the Llanelli–All Blacks game, Huw Llewelyn Davies makes this observation. 'I'm not sure we can say that the actual broadcasting of the Lions games themselves was a watershed in rugby broadcasting, but it is true to say that because of the success of the Lions, rugby became bigger and bigger in terms of being a television sport.' And the experience of the television rugby viewing fan would be far closer in those days to the experience of the fan viewing live at the rugby ground than it is today.

So a process seems to be forming. High post-'71 expectations, fuelled by a new interest from television, was elevating the Llanelli game before it started. Max Boyce contributed to that process when the famous victory was secured as, indeed, did the Groggs caricature of Delme. Other factors kicked-in to accelerate the process even further.

The impact of the All Blacks defeat was shared by people not only from Llanelli itself. Maybe this is felt most acutely by those players who were brought into the team in the months or weeks before the game. Tommy David was the one who lived the furthest away. 'When I got back to Pontypridd, it was amazing how many people were coming up to congratulate me and ask about the victory. I had loads of phone calls at home and people used to call round all the time. They wanted to share in the victory as genuine Pontypridd supporters. It obviously meant as much to them as it did to Llanelli fans.'

J.J. Williams and Chico Hopkins share the same feelings and Roger Davies has already mentioned his reception back at the Uplands Rugby Club in Swansea on the night of the game. Barry Llewelyn would have witnessed the same response in Tenby. Huw Llewelyn Davies mentions another factor. 'It's still true to say that Llanelli is the club that represents the Welsh speakers. In 1972 Carwyn would have been a prominent figure in that Welsh-speaking world. Welsh-speaking Wales would have identified with that win as being one for their club. The club has that affinity with Welsh-speaking Wales to this day, even though it might not be as strong as it used to be.'

Therefore, through the medium of broadcasting, geography and language, the impact of 9–3 was felt over a much wider area. There were also factors that could be considered as more pure rugby, as Peter Stead explains. 'Let's not underestimate the effect that an All Black visit would have in those days either. It was massive. Added to that was how big the club structure was in Wales with up to 50 games in a season. So, the affinity between fan and club was quite deep-rooted. When your club won like Llanelli did, the feeling would be deep. But other clubs would want to share in it too.'

One indication as to how the whole perception within the club scene of an All Blacks tour has changed, is to hear the reaction of a modern-day player. Today's superstar wing at Llanelli, George North, recalls hearing of Llanelli's '72 victory. 'I remember hearing about the victory a few years ago, when I was in my mid-teens. My reaction was two-fold. Firstly thinking, well done them, what an achievement and then stopping to think, why on the earth would Llanelli be playing the All Blacks anyway?' That sums it all up. Sixteen-year-old George left his home in Anglesey to study A Levels at Llandovery College. He received a joint Llanelli Academy Scholarship and a Carwyn James Scholarship. The legacy continues.

As with linking Carwyn James and George North, it could be argued that the old and the new came together in 1972 as well, with both giving the best they had to offer at the same time. Both traditions had a champion: Carwyn could be seen as being progressive and Delme traditional. And both shared each others values too. Carwyn was a man ahead of his time. He wanted to change things, to develop, to progress, to challenge the system in order to move the game on to the next era. Delme stood for other values and was prepared to forgo all the honours he'd won in the international game in order to achieve the one local success on a pitch in front of his home crowd. Both outlooks needed each other. Carwyn needed Delme as much as Delme needed Carwyn.

That balance is something rare and is something essential for a team to move forward. Clubs today face this challenge to get the balance right, including the present-day Llanelli. Today it's the need to get the balance right between heritage and business. One can devalue the other, one can be emphasised at the expense of the other. Even in remembering the 1972 victory itself, Llanelli haven't always got it right. The reaction has swung from not giving the players the proper recognition years after the win, to being far too self-indulgent and giving the event a greater significance than it should get.

When the twenty-fifth anniversary of 1972 came around, the club decided that it didn't want to mark the occasion officially. But, the players decided that they would meet and celebrate their achievement. Grav, at that time, was the club's president, and felt awkward about being in the middle, between team and club. He argued the players' case and with a few days to go, the club said they wanted to honour the team after all. But, the committee were told exactly where they could go with their last-minute gesture, and the players did their own thing.

For years after that, however, it has been felt that the club has lived on that one date and that one date alone. Both fans and club have seemingly lived in the past, with 1972 becoming their 1066 or 1945 or 1282. On a television debate after the series *The Story of Wales*, Swansea historian, Chris Williams, made a point about an attitude the Welsh can have towards their history. It can be applied to any aspect of Welsh history, including such an integral part of that history as rugby is, as well as that single game in '72. He said there was now a need '… to no longer be enthralled to the past, no longer to be concerned to define Wales by those elements in the past we want to prioritise and select.' Llanelli has chosen to select 31 October 1972 and prioritise it, but to the extent that this one event has defined everything about the club. But this in no way takes away from the victory itself. Yesterday and today need to be balanced, as they were in 1972.

It's often asked how the All Blacks themselves view the impact of that one victory against them, and the way it has been remembered since. The assumption is that they must find it strange that we rejoice so much over one win so long ago. Bryan Williams, however, doesn't see it like that at all. 'I don't think that the victory is celebrated too much at all. That's what you do at special occasions, is to remember them and celebrate them. That was a special achievement by Llanelli. I don't mind the way they remember that at all. In a way, as a sportsman, you don't mind being part of a great sporting achievement, even if you were at the wrong end of it. That's also how I felt about the Baa-Baa's try against us on the same tour. It was my kick that Phil Bennett gathered to start the move and I made a coat hanger tackle on J.P.R. when the ball came to him. So, that try wouldn't have happened without me! I say that all the time, because I want to be part of it. It's the same attitude to what happened at Stradey.'

From a fans' point of view, there's no doubt that the thrill of the day was largely due to being so close to it: that cauldron, that amphitheatre of passion and fanaticism which we were all part of. There's no doubt that being able to sit so close to the action and then being allowed to run onto the pitch in joyful celebration, was an integral part of the whole experience. There is no way it could have been enjoyed with the same intensity and passion if it were watched under the excessive, sterile, crowd control conditions of today. Thank goodness we could watch it as we did.

But, the last word must go to the players themselves. They have no doubt, certainly the ones from Llanelli, where the impact of their victory comes for them. It's best summed up by Gareth Jenkins, Delme Thomas and Phil Bennett, who, independently of each other, all used the same phrases, with the same emotion, when asked why they thought '72 is remembered as it is. And thousands of others will identify with their opinions. It was the pure rugby achievement of beating the All Blacks, of course. But, more than that, for them it was the fact that the victory was achieved by men from a small working-class town with roots in the traditional heavy industries integral to the shaping of Wales that made it significant, and that's what made it special.

Also available from Y Lolfa:

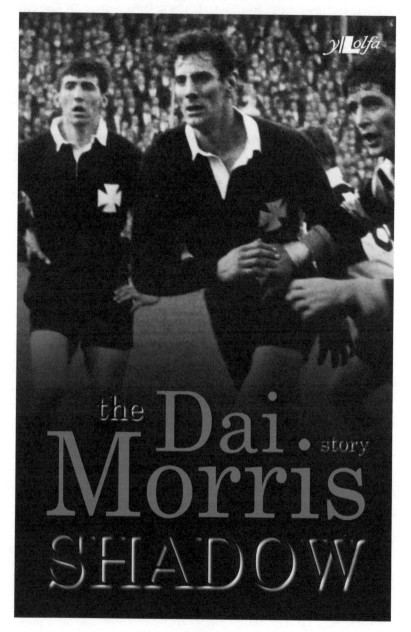

£9.95

'Exposing the truth about the Regions and the demise of rugby in the Welsh Valleys'

Lynn Howells

Despite the Knockbacks

Introductions by Graham Henry and Neil Jenkins

£9.95

Simon
EASTERBY
Easter's Rising

£9.95

LYNN DAVIES

hard men of WELSH RUGBY

yLolfa

£7.95

Who Beat the All Blacks? is just one of a
whole range of publications from Y Lolfa.
For a full list of books currently in print, send
now for your free copy of our new full-colour
catalogue. Or simply surf into our website

www.ylolfa.com

for secure on-line ordering.

yLolfa

TALYBONT CEREDIGION CYMRU SY24 5HE
e-mail ylolfa@ylolfa.com
website www.ylolfa.com
phone (01970) 832 304
fax 832 782